Coastal Navigation

COASTAL NAVIGATION

A Programmed Learning Course

Second edition

Gerry Smith, B.Ed., Yachtmaster

ADLARD COLES LIMITED
GRANADA PUBLISHING
London Toronto Sydney New York

Published by Granada Publishing in Adlard Coles Limited, 1981
Second Edition
First published by Elek Books Limited, 1977

Granada Publishing Limited
Frogmore, St. Albans, Herts AL2 2NF
and
3 Upper James Street, London W1R 4BP
Suite 405, 4th Floor, 866 United Nations Plaza, New York, NY 10017 USA
Q164 Queen Victoria Buildings, Sydney, NSW 2000, Australia
100 Skyway Avenue, Toronto, Ontario, Canada M9W 3A6
PO Box 84165, Greenside, 2034 Johannesburg, South Africa
61 Beach Road, Auckland, New Zealand.

Copyright © Gerry Smith 1977 and 1981

ISBN 0 229 11655 8

Printed and bound in Great Britain by William Clowes (Beccles) Limited,
Beccles and London

Granada®
Granada Publishing®

Introduction

Truk is a community in the Pacific and of its inhabitants, the Trukese, it is claimed that:

'Voyages spanning over one hundred miles of open ocean are still made in sailing canoes, and longer ones were made in the past. The destination is often a tiny dot of land less than a mile across, and visible from any distance only because of the height of those coconut trees which may grow in its sandy soil. From a canoe, virtually at the level of the ocean's surface, even a forested island is visible only three or four miles away. To ensure that the travellers will come close enough to their destination to sight it after covering miles of empty ocean, with shifting winds and currents, the crew usually rely on one of their number who has been trained in a variety of traditional techniques by an older master navigator, usually a relative of his. These techniques do not even include a compass . . .*

The Trukese need very little other than their own intuition and traditional guidance in order to make their destination. They obviously know the departure position which was Truk and they would, through past experience, have a good idea where they would end up. It's what they do on voyage which is the interesting part. Do they steer by noting the general direction of the wind or perhaps the motion of the waves? Do they use the age-old techniques of using the information they have gained of the movements of the stars, sun and moon? Or are their methods really very crude and extremely dangerous?

The wise European sailor would not consider sailing the sea without certain instruments, of which the compass is of top priority. It is certain that he would not place himself in a situation where he was very unsure about where he was, or indeed where he would be unable to predict the track which his voyage would make over the sea. In other words he has got to know where he is and where he will be in time to come, and the way he does this is to be able to fix his position while he is on passage.

It is highly improbable that the majority of us have master navigators as members of our family who can 'turn to' and teach us the methods needed to navigate successfully. In that respect we are not as lucky as the Trukese. The best we can do is to search out a good teacher who can give us an insight into the underlying processes which we need in order to understand the principles involved.

There is no known adequate substitute for a very good teacher, but there are some ways in which the absence of first rate tuition may be only part hindrance. A book such as this should help considerably.

This publication 'teaches' because it gives you the chance to make mistakes and then guides you to a better understanding of the causes of them. If you are very competent it is possible that you can do the programme in a

* Thomas Gladwin, 'Culture and logical process', in Ward Goodenough (ed.), *Explorations in Cultural Anthropology; Essays in Honour of George Peter Murcock (New York, McGraw-Hill, 1964).*

shorter time than usual because you are not required to do all the pages; you obviously will not make many mistakes. But if you do get wrong answers – and everyone does at some time or other – the course is designed to channel you to 'back-up' material which should help to set you back on the correct course. Incidentally this programme has been tested on a population of evening class students representing many occupations. They were complete beginners which no previous knowledge of the subject. The average time taken to work through the text and associated exercises was about 15 hours. If you take longer to get it finished don't worry because it is after all only an average time. The all-important consideration which should govern your work is that you understand what you are doing.

In the light of the experience of the experimental try-out you will find that this programme helps considerably with any evening classes attended, or, if you are already part-experienced, it will offer a valuable means of revising basic principles. And for all those who cannot attend live courses – many people find that through business or professional commitments a regular 'stint' every week at evening class is out of the question – this book should fill a particular need.

Fundamental principles only are taught in these pages. No claim is made that this publication represents a thoroughly comprehensive informational account on all matters relating to coastal navigation. Wherever possible the ideas have been simplified to make for better understanding. Several well-known text books have been surveyed during the writing of this work and the terminology used here is offered as an acceptable pattern as used by many people.

This book has been written with the needs of the small boat sailor very much in mind and the material is focussed on the person who frequently sails coastwise around the shores in a boat no longer than, say, a 30-footer. Sea-anglers and sub-aqua sportsmen, in addition to sailors, should get sound advice and teaching from it. The only starting qualifications this programme asks of you is that you can add, subtract, multiply and divide simply numbers and that you will accept that the earth is, roughly speaking, spherical.

Finally, learning navigation involves an active theory and practice link-up. You should get to know the sea and know that you know it. The only way of doing this is to get some sea-time in with an experienced navigator; then you will realise the value of the theory you have studied to get.

Take a look at the next page which outlines the programme before starting the study course which begins on page 1

CONTENTS

If you haven't already done so please read the Introduction and then start the programme on page 1.

UNIT 1 The Earth

A practice chart, parallel ruler, dividers, a soft pencil and a rubber are all that is needed to begin this course.

The chart used is instructional chart No 5050 Falmouth to Plymouth. The parallel ruler should be at least 12 inches long and it may be completely plain or marked with a protractor. After you have finished any form of chart-marking with the pencil the lines or figures should be rubbed off (hence the need for a soft pencil – about 2B – so that the paper isn't imprinted and permanently scored).

You will be asked questions and given a selection of answers, one correct and the others incorrect. You should select the correct answer. Always try to work it out and do not guess. If you can resolve the problem by thinking about it then you will make sound progress and not be required to read every page.

But don't worry if you get the wrong answer because the course is designed to put you right and give the necessary extra practice.

Now turn to page 3

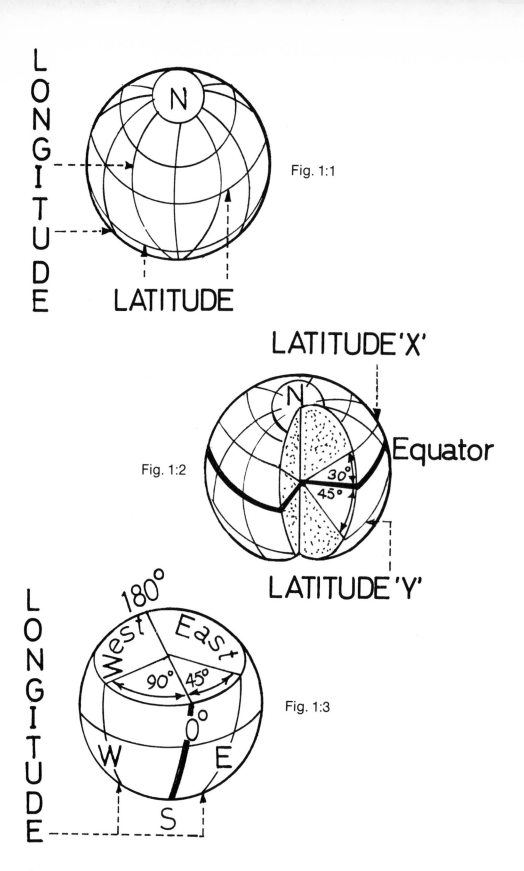

Fig. 1:1

Fig. 1:2

Fig. 1:3

The earth is divided up by imaginary lines which are called LATITUDE and LONGITUDE (Fig. 1:1).

Lines of Latitude are circles round the earth set parallel to the Equator and they are measured through an arc of 90 degrees (90°) North or 90° South of this line (Fig. 1:2). The parallel of Latitude marked with an 'X' would be recorded as 30° North because it is North of the Equator. Latitude 'Y' is therefore 45° South.

The lines of Longitude, which all pass through the North and South Poles, are measured from the Greenwich Meridian. This is a line which passes through the North Pole, through Greenwich in London and then the South Pole. In Fig. 1:3 the Greenwich Meridian is marked as 0°. You can see that Longitude 'E' is recorded as 45° East because it measures East from the Greenwich Meridian. Longitude 'W' is 90° West.

Turn to page 5

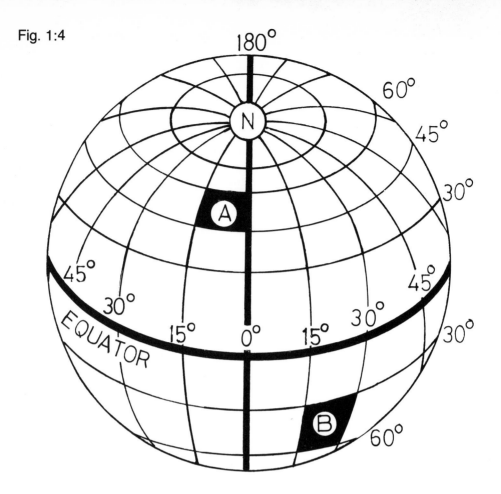

By using a system of cross references any area on the earth can be specified. For example in Fig. 1:4 an area bordered by Latitude 45°N and 60°N and Longitude 0° and 15°W has been shaded in and marked 'A'.

Name the two lines of Latitude and the two lines of Longitude which border the shaded area 'B'.

(When you think you have the answer select the one which you consider to be correct from the two given below and then turn to the page indicated next to your selection)

Latitude	**30°S**	**Latitude**	**60°S**	
Longitude	**0° W**	**Longitude**	**15° W**	. . . *page 7*

Latitude	**30° S**	**Latitude**	**60° S**	
Longitude	**15° E**	**Longitude**	**30° E**	. . . *page 9*

Fig. 1:5

If you are in area 'B' you must be in a Latitude
which is South and a Longitude which is
East.

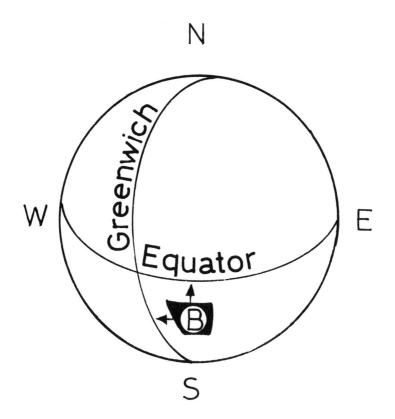

X

You have made an attempt and come up with the wrong answer, but there's no need to worry because many people make that particular error.

Many students get confused about the directional aspects – whether the Latitude is North or South, or perhaps they mistake East for West Longitudes.

Try to imagine yourself to be on the Equator. If you have to move southwards to reach area 'B' then it is in sourthern Latitudes. Also, if you are on the Meridian of Greenwich and you have to move eastwards to reach 'B' then that area will be in eastern Longitudes. Refer to Fig. 1:5.

Move on to page 9

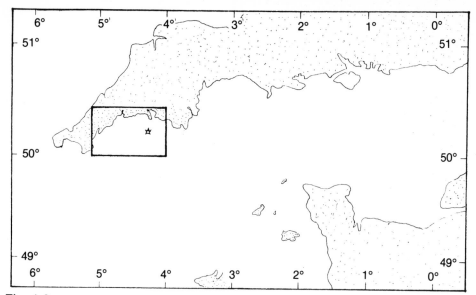

Fig. 1:6

Fig. 1:7

Another technique for plotting a position is to use the dividers and parallel rulers simultaneously. In Fig. 1:7 the ruler has been lined up with the Latitude scale and the dividers have been used to read off the Longitude.

Fig. 1:8

Notice that on the practice chart the grid lines are conveniently placed to help with position plotting.

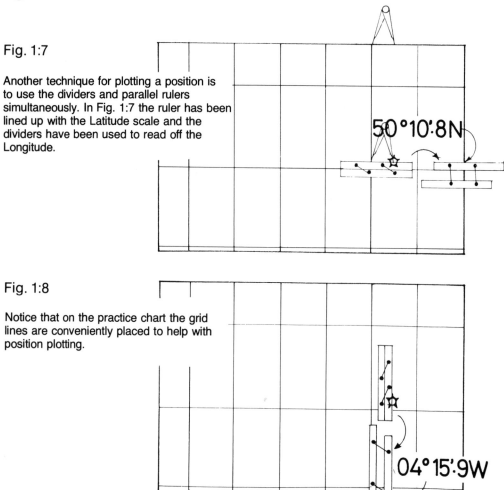

Previously we have been thinking in terms of degrees as units of measurement. Well, there are 60 parts to a degree and these are called MINUTES. Look at the practice chart. The area which it borders is within the parallels of Latitude 49°59'N (49 degrees 59 minutes) and 50°24'.7N (50 degrees 24 minutes and seven-tenths of a minute). The lines of Longitude are 04°01'W and 05°06'W. Fig. 1:6 shows how the chart may be seen as a portion of a larger area.

Having seen how to identify an area we move on and plot a position. By using just two reference lines, one of Latitude and the other of Longitude, an exact point may be marked on the chart. For example, if the location of the Eddystone Light House is required it can be found very easily. Place the parallel rulers in line with the top or bottom edge of the chart (or any grid line which runs across it – such as the one going horizontally at Latitude 50°10'N) and 'walk' them until an edge is touching the small star which marks the Light House. Then read along this edge and see where it cuts the Latitude scale. This will be 50°10'.8N (see Fig. 1:7).

The Longitude may be found in the same way but with the rulers placed vertically in line with either right or left edge of the chart (or suitable grid line such as 04°30'W) before they are 'walked' across to the Light House. The Longitude is 04°15'.9W and this is shown in Fig. 1:8.

The position of the Eddystone Light House would therefore read 50°10'.8N 04°15'.9W.

Always use the same edge of the ruler throughout a Latitude or Longitude plot. In other words the edge which is placed on the side of the chart should be the one which actually touches the light house. This will reduce the chances of inaccuracy due to distortion in the ruler edges.

Incidentally, if you are in any doubt about which Longitude you are in, East or West, look at the bottom of the chart because there will be the information you require.

Which of the following positions is the correct one for the Pier Light at Looe?

50°21'N   04°27'W . . . *page 11*
50°20'N   04°27'W . . . *page 13*

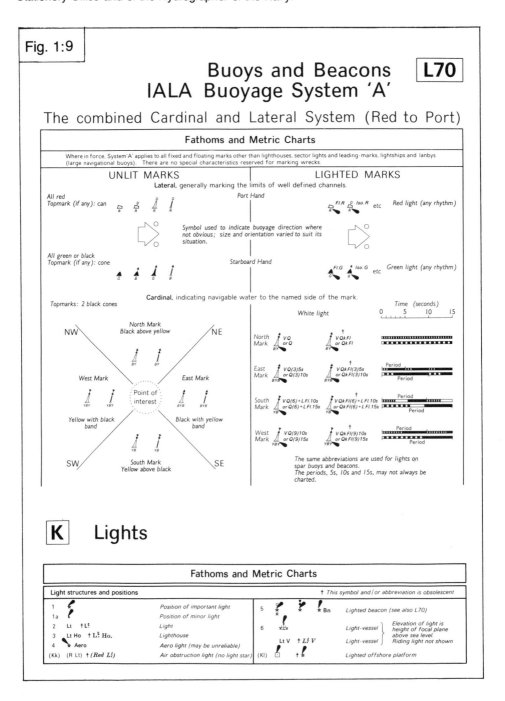

The publication from which these excerpts were taken, a booklet catalogued as Chart 5011, is a 'must' for anyone who is learning coastal navigation. It gives symbols and abbreviations for Fathoms as well as Metric charts. In particular you should look at the section on Dangers.

☑ *Very good*

You seem to have a clear idea of how to plot a position. There will be a considerable amount of this to do in the future. However, it is possible that at this point you are getting tired of the programme. If this is so then you should stop now and carry on at a later date. If you are enjoying the experience then press on.

As with all maps it is necessary that symbols are marked on charts. Most charts incorporate some symbols which are similar to those used on ordinary maps and some such as hills and buildings are well known. But as you may expect there are on charts mostly symbols and abbreviations which are particular to the sea and a selection of these is illustrated in Fig. 1:9 on the opposite page.

On some of these symbols there is a small circle which represents the actual position of the object or mark. Because of the scale of some charts objects such as buoys or light vessels may appear considerably larger than they really are, so the small circle specifies a more exact location (look at the Light Vessel in Fig. 1:9). If there is no small circle then the actual centre of the object is the position. All the symbols used are sensible and with applied common sense they may be recognised.

The units used in mapping or charting depths of the sea are given in the chart heading or legend. On our practice chart metres are used. On some other charts fathoms are still used (1 fathom = 6 feet). Depths may be shown as either contour lines or numbers, or both.

The features of the sea and the shoreline alter constantly; for example ships are wrecked, buoys are moved due to shifting sands creating new sandbanks, and the characteristics of lighthouses sometimes change. Navigational hazards like these must be noted on the chart, and the necessary corrections may be found in the Admiralty publication 'Notices to Mariners', which can be obtained at chart agents, Customs Houses, harbour offices etc. You can either pay a chart agent to correct your charts or you can do it yourself; it is best to make a note of the date and number of the relevant Admiralty Notice to Mariners in the bottom left-hand corner of the chart (if the correction is permanent, use waterproof ink, if not then pencil is better): e.g. 1980-1396 shows Notice to Mariners number 1396 of 1980.

There are no corrections listed on the practice chart. Before you attempt the next problem have a good look over it, and study the features shown.

What depth of water is there in position 50°11'N   04°18'W, and what is the quality of the bottom?

57 metres, fine sand (fs) . . . *page 15*
34 metres, rock (R) . . . *page 15*

Fig. 1:10

If you are in any doubt about whether the Longitude is East or West look at the bottom of a chart

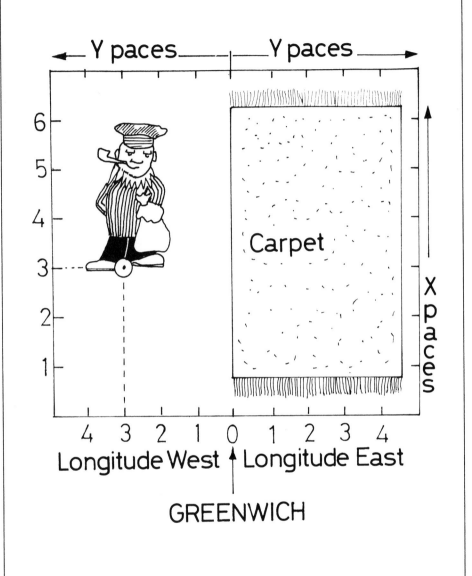

The position which you have selected would set you to the south of Looe Island.

Always double check your answers. You won't get them exactly the same as the book at every attempt but you should get them very close.

If you are still a bit confused about plotting positions then it may help you if you were to imagine that the sea is represented as a room. In fact, try to compare the chart to a room.

In Fig. 1:10 the 'X' wall is marked off in paces and so is the 'Y' wall. The edge of the carpet may be regarded as the Greenwich Meridian and the 'old salt' in the diagram would therefore be in a position Latitude 3 paces North and Longitude 3 paces West.

Turn back to page 9 and think it out again

MERCATOR PROJECTION

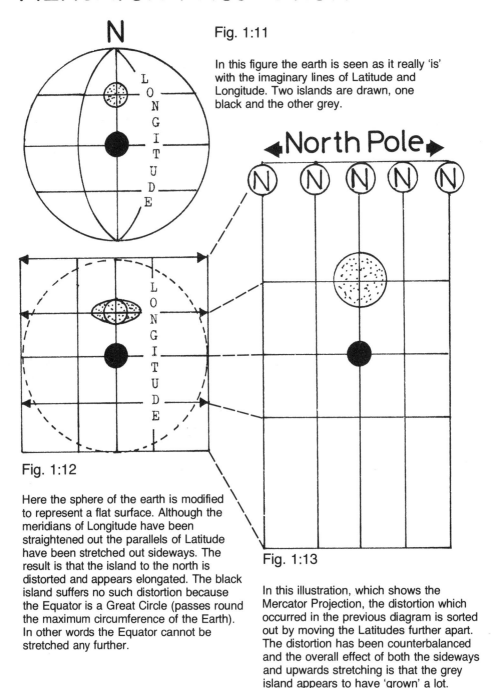

Fig. 1:11

In this figure the earth is seen as it really 'is' with the imaginary lines of Latitude and Longitude. Two islands are drawn, one black and the other grey.

Fig. 1:12

Here the sphere of the earth is modified to represent a flat surface. Although the meridians of Longitude have been straightened out the parallels of Latitude have been stretched out sideways. The result is that the island to the north is distorted and appears elongated. The black island suffers no such distortion because the Equator is a Great Circle (passes round the maximum circumference of the Earth). In other words the Equator cannot be stretched any further.

Fig. 1:13

In this illustration, which shows the Mercator Projection, the distortion which occurred in the previous diagram is sorted out by moving the Latitudes further apart. The distortion has been counterbalanced and the overall effect of both the sideways and upwards stretching is that the grey island appears to have 'grown' a lot.

The further north(or south) you go, the more the Mercator Projection distorts until, at the North or South poles, the distortion is such that the Pole tends to stretch from one edge of the chart to the other. Thus all the grid lines from the bottom to the top of the chart point towards north (in Fig. 1:13 shown as the symbol N).

57 metres fine sand is right. 34 metres rock is wrong.

However, the fact that you have progressed this far means that you generally understand the principles so this mistake, if made, may be considered a minor discrepancy.

You will recall that there are 60 minutes in 1 degree and you should now learn that each of these minutes is equal to 1 nautical mile. Whole minutes and fractions of minutes are marked on the chart. On our particular practice chart each minute is divided into 10 parts, each part being $\frac{1}{10}$ mile.

Just to complete the picture we can state that there are 10 cables in 1 nautical mile so each tenth equals 1 cable. From now all nautical miles will be referred to as 'miles'. There is some difference between land (statute) miles and nautical miles. A nautical mile is 6076 feet but a land mile is 5280 feet. This difference does not concern us here and throughout the programme we shall 'think nautical'.

Charts, which are flat surfaces, are designed to represent a curved surface (the earth). Because of this alteration a distortion occurs and the end result is that the Latitude scale is affected. For this reason the LATITUDE SCALE SHOULD ALWAYS BE USED FOR MEASURING DISTANCES. You will remember that the Latitude scale is the vertical scale (the right and left hand edges of the chart).

It is important to make sure that the Latitude scale nearest the area of the chart which is being 'worked on' is the part used for measuring distances. For example in Fig. 1:14 the distance between △ and ☉ is to be measured. The way to do this is to open up the dividers so that a point is on each of the marks and then see how far the distance is on the Latitude scale nearest the area of operations. You will see that the distance works out as 1.2 miles.

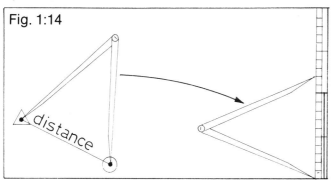

Fig. 1:14

Now let's return to the practice chart. If we wanted to measure the distance between Looe Light and Polperro Light the dividers should be opened so that a point is placed in the centre of the two small stars. Keep the dividers opened at the same distance and transfer them to the Latitude scale 'in line' across the chart. The distance is 2.7 miles. You should check this figure.

Read the notes on the opposite page if you want to understand more thoroughly the reason for the Latitude scale distortion which was discussed on this page. Otherwise carry on to page 16.

Summary

a) A position may be plotted by using cross references of Latitude and Longitude.

b) Charts have 'Longitude East of Greenwich' or 'Longitude West of Greenwich' printed on them.

c) Charts use symbols. The position of an object is a small circle marked on its symbol. If there is no circle then the centre of the symbol marks its position.

d) Because charts are really two-dimensional maps which represent a curved surface there is a distortion effect which is shown in the Latitude scale. DISTANCES ARE MEASURED ON THIS SCALE ONLY.

e) There are 60 minutes in 1 degree; 1 minute equals 1 mile; there are 10 cables in 1 mile.

f) Always measure distances on the Latitude scale nearest to the area in which you are operating.

g) Chart corrections have to be made from time to time. These are found in Admiralty Notices to Mariners.

Do the exercises on the next page.

Excercise 1A

In all the exercises, where nothing else is specified, use the practice chart 5050.

Plot the position of the following

a) St Ewe Church (near the grid line 04°50'W)
b) Black Rock Beacon (off St Anthony Head)
c) Conspicuous mark on Gribbin Head (SW of Fowey Harbour)
d) Carne Beacon (north of Nare Head – near Gerrans Bay)
e) Centre of the Tidal Diamond ⬦ near St Anthony Head

Exercise 1B

Measure the distances between the following

a) St Anthony Head Light House to Carne Beacon
b) Carne Beacon to St Ewe Church
c) St Ewe Church to Killyvarder Rock Beacon (in Tywardreath Bay)
d) Killyvarder Rock Beacon to Tywardreath Church
e) Tywardreath Church to Looe Church (if your dividers are not large enough to measure, draw a line between the two places and measure in sections)

It always pays to check the answers. Remember, always measure distances on the LATITUDE S nearest to the area of operations.
                      C
                      A
                      L
                      E

Exercise 1C

Assume that in 1980 the Admiralty Notices to Mariners number 1122 the following information was given about chart 5050:

1122 ENGLAND, S. COAST – Plymouth Sound
Tower demolished 50°21.8'N   04°08'.5W

How would you correct your chart and record the correction?

Answers overleaf. Your answers may not be exactly the same as those officially listed but you should be able to get them to within 0.1' when measuring distance and to within the same margin when position plots are being done.

Answers: Exercise 1A

a) Latitude 50°16'.8N   Longitude 04°50'.3W
b) Latitude 50°08'.7N   Longitude 05°01'.9W
c) Latitude 50°19'N   Longitude 04°40'.3W
d) Latitude 50°12'.6N   Longitude 04°55'.6W
e) Latitude 50°08'.5N   Longitude 05°01'.5W (Incidentally all the tidal stream diamonds are plotted and the position registered in the tables which are just under the chart heading).

Answers: Exercise 1B

a) 5.4 miles
b) 5.3 miles
c) 6.6 miles
d) 1.1 miles
e) 9.2 miles

Answers: Exercise 1C

First of all the actual tower has to be crossed out thus ⊥⊙ and then the date and number of the correction added to the others (if any) listed at the bottom left-hand corner of the chart. So, on your copy of 5050 you should have written: 1980–1122.

Rating score *(treat each exercise separately)*

5 correct answers   – Plain sailing
4 correct   – Just sailing
3 correct   – Return to page 6
Less than 3 correct   – Re-read Unit 1

If you don't have to return to a previous page carry on to the next unit

UNIT 2 The Course Steered

If the work on this programme becomes boring, or tiring, you should stop doing it and have a break. You can always return to it later on and by such time you will probably find you can work with a clearer brain.

However, this unit should not take you very long – just a few minutes in fact. During the 'try-out' of this programme on evening class students most people thought this unit was very simple. Do it and see what you think.

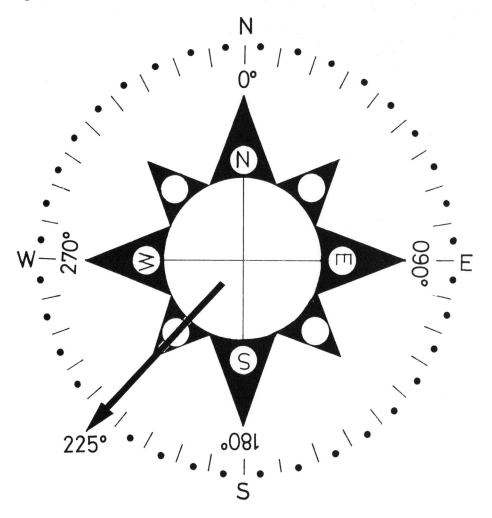

Of all the sophisticated marine equipment available to the small boat sailor the compass is probably the simplest but certainly one of the most necessary instruments.

In its basic form it is a magnetic needle which points towards the north.

In fact, what we really see when we look at the compass is the 'compass card' under which are several magnetic needles. This card is pivoted on a point so that it rotates freely and it is usually floating in a bowl of alcohol. This prevents it from pitching around too much when the boat moves.

A simple form of compass card appears in Fig. 2:1. As with the compass rose on a chart the degrees are marked from 0° through to 360°.

North is 0°. Which direction does 225° indicate?

North-west . . . *page 23*
South-east . . . *page 25*
South-west . . . *page 27*

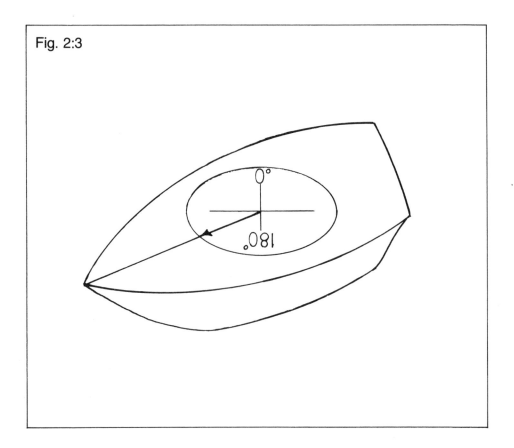

Fig. 2:2

Fig. 2:3

Wrong.

North-west would be 315°. Due West is 270° and therefore North-west would be 270° + 45° which is 315°. 225° is South-west.

To help to fix this idea in mind consider where you are as you read these words. If you are standing indoors then identify the north aspect of the room and, from there, imagine a huge compass marked on the ground.

The direction faced can be found by extending a line from you to cut the edge of the compass rose. To avoid confusion this line is marked by a single arrow head (Fig. 2:2).

At sea the boat cannot be put in the centre of a great compass but a small compass can be installed on the vessel. The situation is the other way round but the principle of the thing does not alter. The main thing to note is that the compass remains steady and the boat does the moving. In Fig. 2:3 is a simplified diagram showing the compass sited on the boat.

Which direction does 135° indicate?

South-east . . . *page 27*
North-west . . . *page 25*

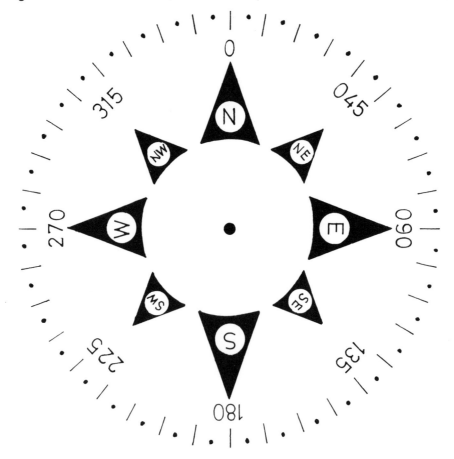

$\boxed{X}$ *Not correct*

It may help to clarify the situation if we go back a step and regard the compass card as a series of 'points'.

The main (cardinal) points are North, South, East and West. The secondary (inter-cardinal) points are North-east, South-east, South-west and North-west.

In all there are 32 points in the circle (360°) and so there are $11\frac{1}{4}°$ in each point $(360° \div 32 = 11\frac{1}{4})$.

Look at the diagram on the opposite page (Fig. 2:4).

Move on to page 27

Fig. 2:5

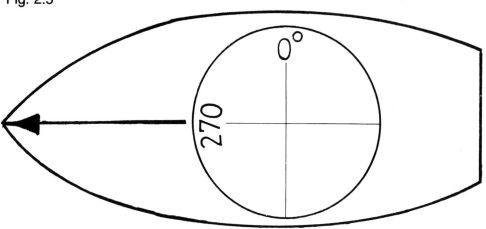

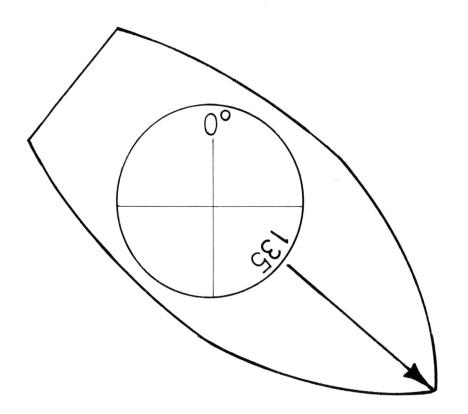

Fig. 2:6

Now that you appear to have the idea of what is where in relation to North we can develop the theme.

When we are at sea instead of saying 'direction faced' we refer to the direction of the boat's head or the COURSE STEERED. The line marking the course steered is always labelled by one arrow head.

In Fig. 2:5 the course steered is 270°.
In Fig. 2:6 the course steered is 135°.

Summary

a) A compass needle points towards the north (0°).
b) A compass is an essential part of a ship's equipment.
c) The term COURSE STEERED refers to the direction in which the boat is heading.
d) The line marking the course steered is labelled by one arrow head.

Do the exercise on page 29 and see how much you know!

Fig. 2:7

If you join the objects referred to in the
questions, the line between them will pass
through the centre of the compass rose. The
course may then be read off.

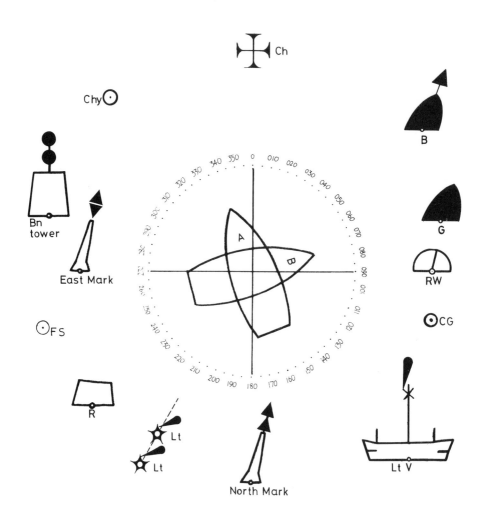

Exercise 2 *(refer to Fig. 2:7 and if necessary to page 10)*

a) In which direction is vessel 'A' heading?

b) What course is vessel 'B' steering?

c) An observer is standing at the Coastguard station (CG) looking towards the beacon tower. Which direction is he facing?

d) What course would a boat have to steer to travel from the light vessel (Lt V) in the direction of the chimney (Chy)?

e) A boat is steering a course from the red port hand buoy (R) to the black starboard hand buoy (B). What is the direction of the boat's head?

f) A craft is on a course with the church (Ch) dead ahead and the north mark buoy dead astern. What course is she steering?

g) Boat 'A' in the diagram decides to alter course and keep the two leading lights in transit and dead ahead. This means that the helmsman, by keeping the two lights in line, knows that he is sailing the craft along a line joining them which extends towards him. What is 'A's new course?

h) Vessel 'B' alters course so that east mark buoy is dead ahead and the red and white spherical buoy (RW) is dead astern. What is her new course and what would be the turning arc through which she must swing to settle on this course (assuming that she alters course to port (left))?

j) A boat is at anchor on a line joining the flagstaff (FS) and the green starboard hand buoy (G). The tide causes her to swing so that she points towards the flagstaff. What is the direction of the boat's head.?

Answers over the page

Answers: Excercise 2

a) 340°
b) 075°
c) 285°
d) 320°
e) 050°
f) 000°
g) 210°
h) New course 270°. Turning arc 165°.
j) 255°

Rating score

9 correct	– Very good
8 correct	– Good
7 correct	– Reasonable
6 correct	– Fair
5 correct	– Poor
Less than 5 correct	– Re-read Unit 2

UNIT 3 The Boat's Track

In the last unit we discussed how the direction of the boat's head and the course steered always relates to the direction of North. In order to comprehend this we imagined, in most instances, the vessel to be in the centre of the compass rose, pivoting and making various angles with 000°.

In this unit we are concerned with a boat actually making way through the sea.

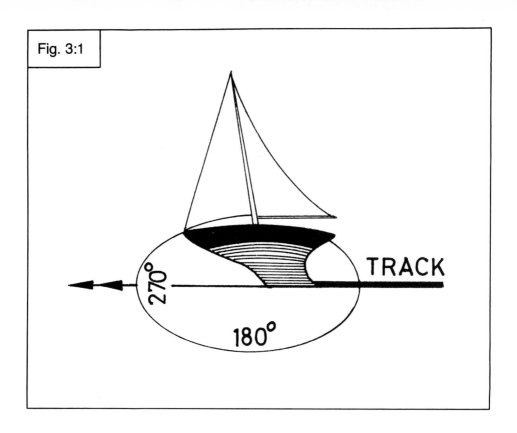

Fig. 3:1

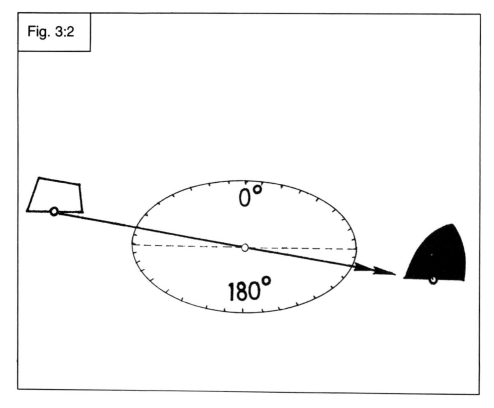

Fig. 3:2

Consider now that the vessel is actually moving along a track. It may help to clarify the meaning if it is imagined that the boat's keel, or centre board, is just scraping the ocean bed but not enough to stop her progress. The mark, or scratch, made by the keel would be the TRACK. (Fig. 3:1).

At first glance it may seem that the course steered must be the same as the track she is making. If there was no wind or tide running then the course and the track would be the same – always providing there was a means of propulsion such as an engine! However the Trukese seamen experienced 'shiftless winds and currents' and these factors often determined that we have to steer a course which is different from the track. Such complications will be dealt with in later units of this book and you would be wise to disregard them at this point.

In Fig. 3:2 a small powered boat is making headway from the port hand (can) buoy to the stardboard hand (conical) buoy. There is no wind or current.)
Which of the following tracks is she making?

110° *. . . page 35*
290° *. . . page 37*

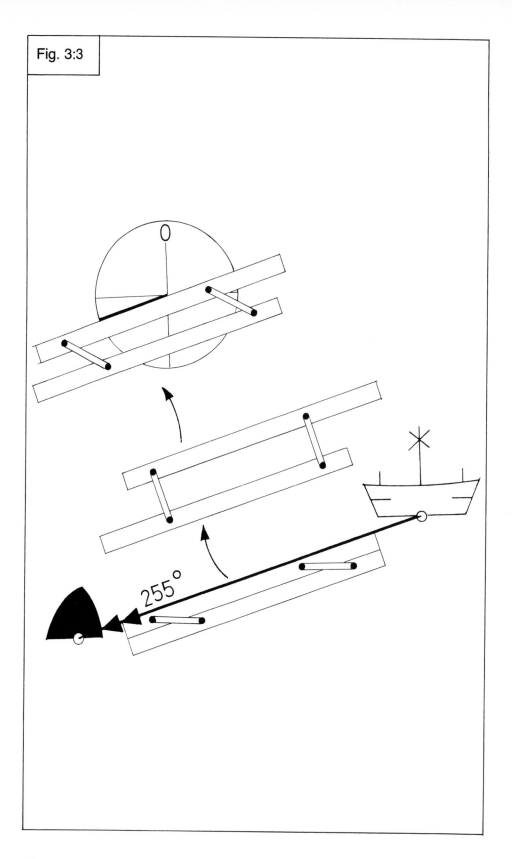

255°

☑ *Good*

You were correct in stating that the track was 110°; to have agreed to 290° would have been to assume that the boat was going backwards (making sternway).

When passage planning the first thing to find out is the track you require (or the Required Track).

To do this you should draw a line from the departure position to the destination making sure that it does not lead you into danger – tide rips, rocks, wrecks, overfalls and the like.* Place the parallel rulers along this line and then 'walk' them over to the centre of the compass rose. The reading obtained would be the REQUIRED TRACK.

For example assume that a boat is travelling from a position at the light vessel to the starboard hand buoy (Fig. 3:3;). In order to find the Required Track a line joining the two positions is drawn. Walk the rulers over to the compass rose and take a reading. The track you require is 255°. The ship's track is always marked with two arrow heads.

Do the following example using the practice chart. (On this chart there are two main circles of degrees on each of the compass roses. Use the *outer* ring; we'll use the inner ring later in the programme.)

If a ship departs from a position 50°06'.5N   05°03'W and is bound for St Anthony Head Light House, which of the following tracks would she require? (Remember to draw a line, marked by two arrow heads, between the two positions.)

215° . . . *page 39*
035° . . . *page 40*

* Tide rips and overfalls are areas in which the sea often behaves in a very rough manner. Steep waves and water tumbling over itself is what normally happens. This type of activity usually occurs near shoal water or headlands. You should refer to 'Symbols and Abbreviations' (see page 10) if you want full information about this sort of phenomenon.

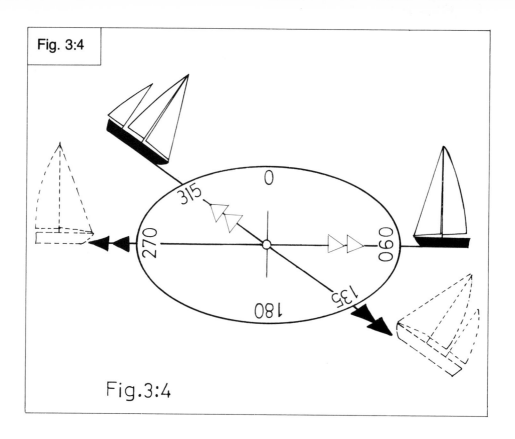

Fig.3:4

X

You have made a very common mistake of reading the track in the opposite direction to the correct one. Most sailors make that error some time in their sailing careers.

When you read off the opposite track you are referring to the reciprocal track. For example in Fig.3:4 the reciprocal of the sloop's track would be 090° and the reciprocal of the ketch's (two masts) track 315°.

Return to page 33

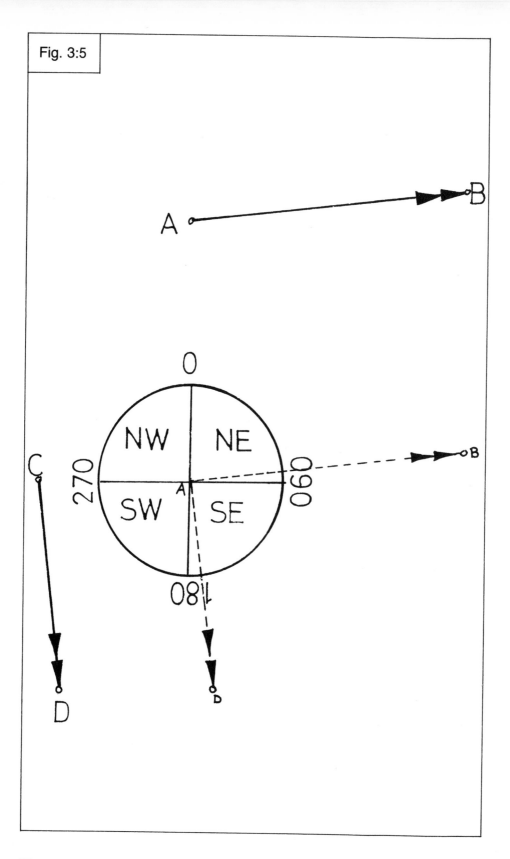

X *035° was the right answer*

It often helps when thinking of tracks or courses to work out which quarter (quadrant) of the compass you are in. For example in Fig. 3:5 a boat sailing from A to B would be on a track which, starting from the centre of the compass, is between 0° and 090°. Similarly a vessel going from C to D would be on a track which, again starting from the centre of the compass, would be somewhere between 090° and 180°. So if you can imagine a compass rose embracing the starting point (departure position) of each track then you are less likely to make a radical error because you have decided upon the quadrant you are in. For example it is highly improbable that you will come out with an answer of 215° when you are sailing in the NE quadrant (0° - 090°).

Page 40 now please

Apart from doing some examples we have just about completed this unit. But first a summary.

a) A vessel's TRACK is the line along which she travels over the ocean bed.
b) When planning the passage the track which you require is the first thing to plot. This should be labelled with two arrow heads which point towards the destination.

Do Exercise 3 on the next page

Exercise 3

Plot the Required Track between the following positions. (There is no wind or tide implied in all the examples.)

Departure	Destination
a) 50° 10′N 04°30′W	− 50° 10′N 04° 20′W
b) 50° 11′N 04° 41′W	− 50° 09′.9N 04° 51′W
c) Plymouth Breakwater Beacon (eastern end of breakwater) (position 50° 20′N 4° 08′.2W)	− Eddystone Light House
d) 50° 12′N 04°14′W	− Looe Light
e) 50° 15′.8N 04° 34′W	− 50° 14′.2N 04°34′W
f) 50° 06′.5N 05°02′W	− St Anthony Head Light House

Answers on page 42

Answers: Exercise 3

a) 090°
b) 260°
c) 208°
d) 317°
e) 180°
f) 020°

Rating Scale

If you have less than 5 correct answers do Unit 3 again.

You are a quarter of the way through the programme. The following Test Piece will examine how much you have learned up till now. Remember to double check all your answers. If you do find out that your answers are not exactly the same as the ones here don't worry too much. However, acceptable limits would be for your answers to be within a margin of 1° where courses are concerned.

Incidently, make sure that your chart is clean; rub out all the previous plots.

Move on to page 43

Test Piece A

This exercise includes a selection of questions which relate to all the work done in the programme so far. If you have any doubt about the accuracy of the answers go back and check them. It's worth doing!

a) What is the position of the fort just behind Plymouth Breakwater?
b) A boat in position 50° 09'N   04° 29'W sails due south for 5 miles. What position does she arrive at?
c) A ship in position 50° 14'.6N   04° 32'.5W takes a sounding (measures the depth of the sea). What is the depth and quality of the bottom?
d) A boat is lying at anchor (from the bow or front) in position 50° 21'N 04° 17'W. There is no tide (slack water) but there is a fresh easterly wind blowing (an easterly wind blows from the east). What would be the direction of the boat's head (i.e. which way will she be pointing)?
e) The wind strengthens even more and she drags her anchor for a cable. What would have been her track?
f) A yacht wishes to sail from 50° 18'.8N   04° 38'W to Looe. In order to avoid offlying dangers she decides to pass through two plotted positions before turning for the harbour. Find the required consecutive tracks she would plot to reach her destination. (No wind or tide).
   1.   50° 18'.4N   04° 30'.4
   2.   50° 19'.5N   04° 24'.5W
   3.   Looe Pierhead Light

Answers on the next page

Answers: Test Piece A

a) 50° 20'N   04° 08'.9W
b) 50° 04'N   04° 29'W
c) 38 metres Rock
d) 090° East
e) Track 270°
f) 1. Required Track 095°
   2. Required Track 074°
   3. Required Track 314°

You should have managed to get all the correct answers. However, taking into account the various possibilities for lapses of concentration, 5 would be acceptable. If you didn't reach this figure re-do Units 1, 2 and 3.

Before moving on to the next unit you may be wise to wait a day or two. It is very often so that to work through the programme without a break upsets the way in which some people learn. Everybody has his own individual preferences – for example, some prefer to work for short periods of about half an hour with frequent intervals of rest, but others would rather work for much longer periods and have a more sustained rest interval.

UNIT 4 Fixing The Boat's Position

There is little sense in starting out on a passage without the necessary means of being able to find out EXACTLY where you are. The ability to find out an actual position forms a sound basis for all coastal navigation.

You can guess where you are, or where you are going to finish up, and this intelligent guess work has an important place to play in the scheme of things. But you must know how to plot an actual or Observed Position before anything else makes sense.

This unit deals with the Observed Position or 'fix'.

Please go to page 47

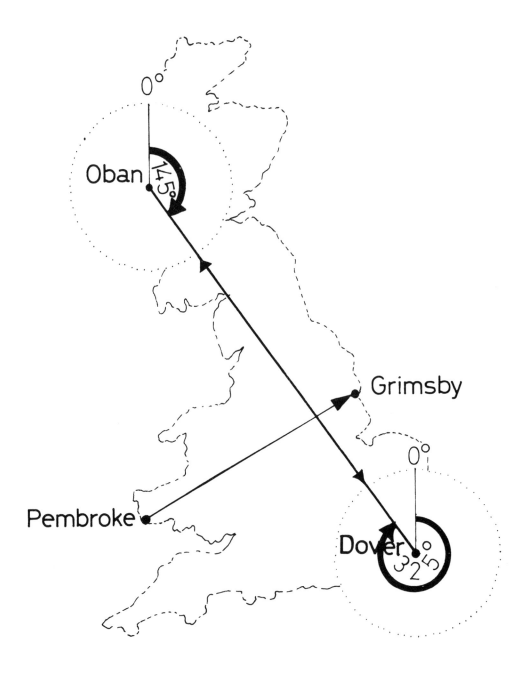

The map in Fig. 4:1 shows a line drawn between Dover and Oban. Now imagine that you are standing in Dover positioned in the centre of a compass rose and that you are facing towards Oban. Oban would be said to bear 325° FROM you. Now imagine that you have turned your back on Oban.

Would your change of direction make any difference to the bearing of 325°?

The answer is No! It does not matter what your heading is because providing you do not move from your location the bearing will remain unchanged.

Thus the bearing of Oban from Dover is 325°. Similarly the bearing of Dover from Oban is 145°. Another way of expressing this is to say that, to an observer in Oban:

Dover bears 145°   OR   Dover 145°

To an observer in Grimsby the town of Pembroke bears

060° . . . *page 49*
240° . . . *page 51*

Fig. 4:2

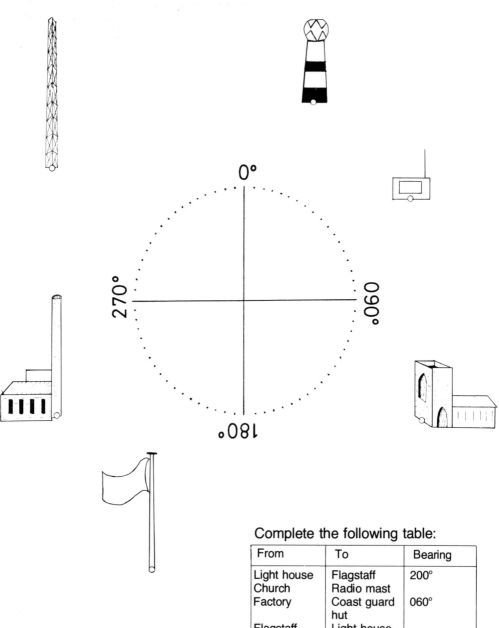

Complete the following table:

From	To	Bearing
Light house	Flagstaff	200°
Church	Radio mast	
Factory	Coast guard hut	060°
Flagstaff	Light house	
Radio mast	Church	123°
Coast guard hut	Factory	

The above examples involve three pairs of objects. So there are three reciprocals (opposites) needed to fill in the missing spaces.

240° is the right answer. The figure you considered as the bearing of Pembroke from Grimsby (060°) is the bearing of Grimsby from Pembroke.

Sometimes it is easy to fall into the trap of reading a reciprocal bearing. For example the opposite of 240° is 060°. It is the exact opposite (reciprocal) and if 180° is taken away from 240° the answer is 060°.

In order to fix the idea of bearings in your mind do the exercise in Fig. 4:2. The answers to this exercise are printed upside down at the bottom of this page. Cover them up before you attempt the questions if you feel that the temptation to look at them is too much for you!

After you have done this exercise please set course for page 47 and re-do the work on it.

From	to	Bearing
Coast Guard hut	Factory	240°
Radio mast	Church	123°
Flagstaff	Light house	020°
Factory	Coast Guard hut	060°
Church	Radio mast	303°
Light house	Flagstaff	200°

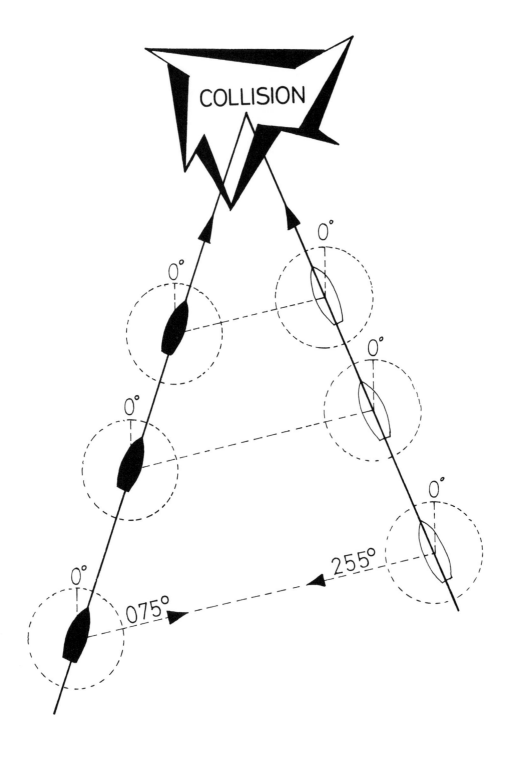

Very good. You seem clear in your mind about the way bearings are read.

Incidentally, it is worth investigating the outcome when two vessels maintain steady bearings of each other. In Fig. 4:3 the black boat finds that the other bears 075° while the white boat finds that the black vessel bears 255°. Assume that both are travelling under power.

Both boats maintain their speeds and courses and after a short period (say 10 minutes) the bearings remain unaltered.

The diagram shows that, if this state of affairs continues, that is if the bearings remain constant, then a collision is very likely.

In order to avoid collision the vessels should alter either courses, or speeds, or both. In point of fact the 'Rules for Preventing Collision at Sea'* determine which boat should do what. In this instance the black vessel should alter course and under normal circumstances she would pass astern of the other.

Instances when a collision will not occur are when both are travelling in the same direction but the vessel ahead is faster than the other, or when they are heading away from each other. Even though the bearings are constant there will not be a collision situation if these two conditions are met.

Page 53 is the next reference

*Information regarding the 'Collision Rules' may be obtained in such publications as *Practical Pilotage* from Adlard Coles Ltd.

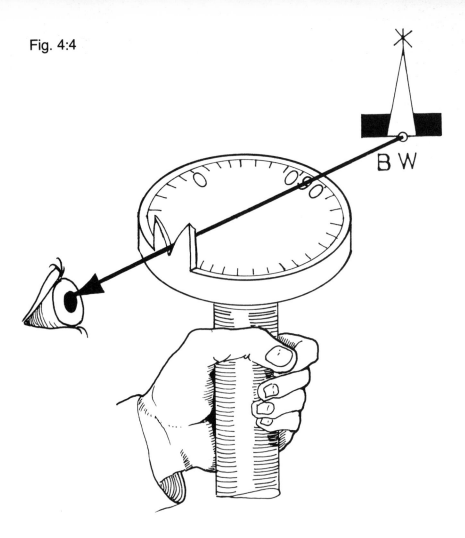

B W

Fig. 4:5

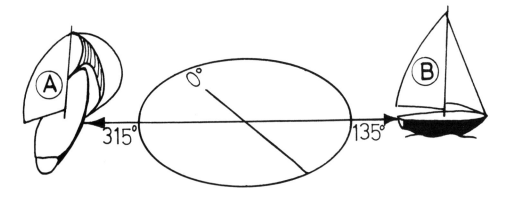

A

B

315° 135°

When bearings are taken* it would be most convenient if a great compass was situated around us; then we would always be in the centre of things and it would be relatively easy to take a bearing of an object.

It would also be helpful if we could get the main boat's compass at height of eye. There are some compasses where this is possible but there are also many more which are mounted in the boat's cockpit and these are usually inaccessible for taking bearings.

So the obvious compromise is adopted – an additional compass is used which we can taken about the boat with us – and this is called a hand-bearing compass.

Fig. 4:4 shows such a compass. This is a simple diagram of a well-known design, but there are other models which are very popular.

The one shown here is very much like a hand-held torch with a small compass placed on top. Sights are taken through the V-shaped eye piece.

The bearing in Fig. 4:4 is 090°. Incidentally the object of which the bearing is taken is called a High Focal Plane Buoy and any reference to it should be treated with caution. Buoys are anchored to the ocean bed, and because the sea level rises and falls the cable which attaches these buoys to their anchorages obviously has to leave some slack. This means that some sideways movement is usual and because of this the position of these buoys is not constant.

However, to continue. In Fig. 4:5 it will be observed that yacht 'A' bears 315° from yacht 'B' and the reciprocal applies (i.e. 'B' bears 135° from 'A').

Carry on to page 55

*The compass is a magnetic instrument. The characteristics of the magnetic forces involved, which give rise to Variation and Deviation, will be disregarded here. The ways in which these are taken into account in practice are dealt with in Units 9 and 11. There is no need to consult these units at present.

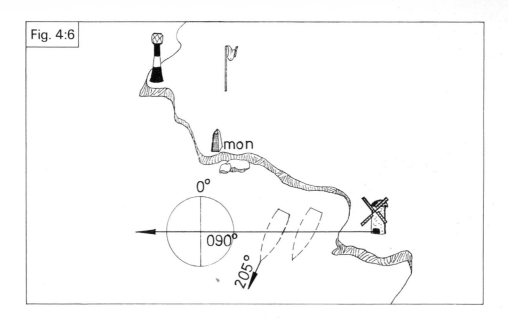

Fig. 4:6

mon

0°

090°

205°

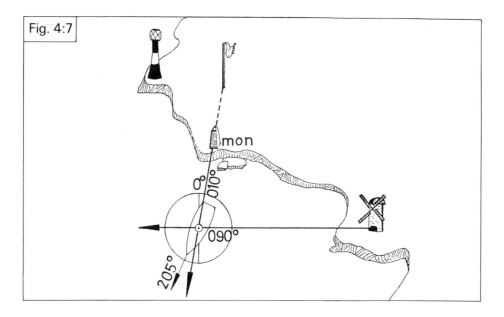

Fig. 4:7

mon

0°

010°

090°

205°

To get an effective transit, the observer should not be more than three times the distance between the landmarks from the nearer one. Transit lines can be used to clear a dangerous area, e.g. in Fig. 4:7 the rocks to the SE of the monument. Many charts show 'leading' marks which provide safe transits for leaving and entering harbour.

Notice that the bearing (Position Line) is marked with an arrow head which points away from the object of which the bearing is taken. In other words it is always pointing towards the person who is taking it.

A bearing gives us a POSITION LINE.

In Fig. 4:6 a ship is heading in a direction which is about 205°. A bearing of the windmill is taken and this turns out to be 090°. This position line informs us that WE MUST BE ON THAT LINE SOMEWHERE.

However, exactly where we are we cannot readily determine until another position line is obtained. As you can see in the illustration, with just one position line we could be in any of the 'ghost' positions (dashed lines).

Two position lines give us a fix at their point of intersection. This fix is called the OBSERVED POSITION and is marked by a circle with a dot ⊙.

A fix can be obtained from a mixture of position lines, found variously from an ordinary compass bearing, a transit (lining up two objects of known position which have been positively identified), or a marine radio beacon. In Fig. 4:7 the monument and flagstaff form a transit.

Radio Bearings

A direction finding radio receiver (D/F set) can produce a bearing on a radio transmitter whose position is known. The D/F set is like a radio with a compass attached to it. As with any radio receiver you tune in to the required station*. You will receive a continuous sound signal. You turn the aerial on the set until the sound fades away (the 'null' point) and at this stage you read off the compass bearing. Some D/F sets have the aerial built inside them so you have to rotate the complete gadget to find 'null'. In the example above, had there been a marine radio beacon set up in the light house, we could have found yet a third position line by using this method. However, the accuracy of the resulting position line can suffer from several errors, as follows:

a) The compass in the D/F set may be either inaccurate, or insufficiently dead beat to give a steady bearing.
b) The signal may be distorted or drowned so that it is difficult to find the 'null'.
c) If the signal crosses a coastline at an acute angle it can suffer refraction (bending).
d) Radio bearings taken at dusk or dawn suffer from distortion.

*The network of marine radio beacons is fully described in *Reed's Nautical Almanac*. In brief, groups of stations on the same frequency transmit morse callsigns for identification at intervals of six minutes, each station within the group being allotted one or more minutes in the six. You can find out a radio beacon's exact frequency, callsign and transmission time if you refer to *Reed's* and other publications. Certain aeronautical radio beacons are also suitable for the mariner. Results improve with practice, but a bearing from a D/F set can seldom be as good as one taken from direct observation.

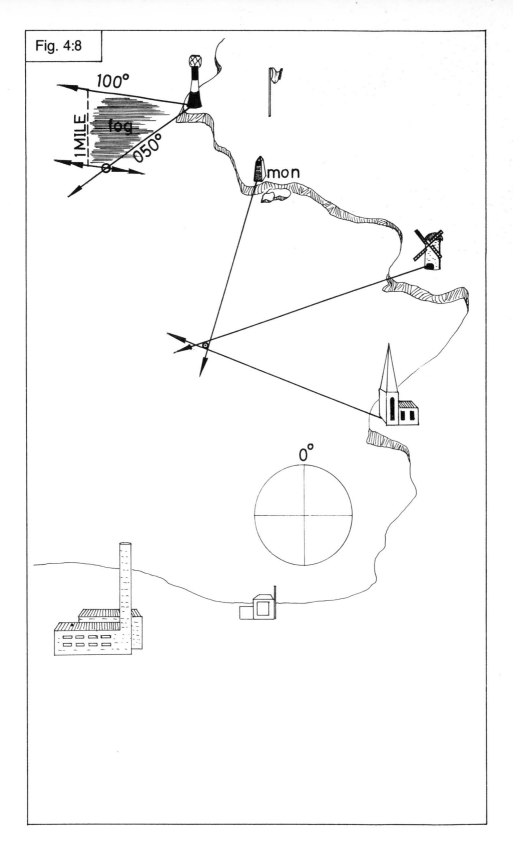

Fig. 4:8

100°

1 MILE

fog

050°

mon

0°

If three position lines can be found then these are likely to be more accurate than just two lines. However, whether this was so would depend upon the angles between the three lines. If these are narrow and are less than about 30°, then the chances are the fix will not be very accurate; two well-angled lines of about 90° would have been more accurate.

In Fig. 4:8 the three lines used are well-angled and the fix would probably have been a good one, always providing that the bearings were taken at approximately the same time and that they were taken with accuracy.

When three lines are used it is often the case that you end up with a 'cocked hat', and this may be seen very clearly in the diagram. If this triangle is relatively small the Observed Position may be assumed to be at the centre.

If there are close-lying hazards such as rocks or shoal ground then the position should be assumed as the corner of the 'cocked hat' nearest the danger.

However, if the 'cocked hat' is unrealistically large then you have made a radical error in taking or plotting the position lines and under these circumstances it is usual to re-do the exercise.

In all the position finding so far, we have used at least two objects for sighting bearings. However, if a boat is making good a known speed and track, but only has one landmark for a bearing, a fix may still be obtained and the method is called a RUNNING FIX.

Refer to the west of the lighthouse in Fig. 4:8. A boat moving due south at 4 knots spots the lighthouse in poor visibility and manages to get a bearing of 100° as fog closes in. A quarter of an hour later she can briefly make out the same lighthouse through the haze; a quick bearing gives 050°. From this information the navigator can work out where he is at the end of the run. He knows that he has travelled 1 mile in 15 minutes (quarter of 4 miles). Both bearings are plotted and the first position line is transferred parallel to itself one mile due south. A transferred position line has two arrowheads at each end. The fix is where the transferred position line and the second position line intersect. Incidentally the distance run, shown as a dashed line (1 mile), could have been plotted anywhere within reason; providing you plot an accurate course direction (in this case due south) and distance, the final position would have come out the same. Try it and see.

If the boat in fog had covered $1\frac{1}{2}$ miles in the example, but still got 050° as the second bearing, would she be further into the bay, further out, or would it not be possible to get a fix?

Turn to page 58

The boat would be further out of the bay because the transferred position line would be half as far again to the south. This would mean that the intersection would have to be further to the west if the second bearing were to be the same.

Summary

a) The direction from us to an object is a bearing.
b) A bearing remains the same no matter which direction you are facing.
c) If the bearing of another vessel remains constant a collision may possibly result.
d) A bearing gives us the POSITION LINE.
e) An intersection of Position Lines gives us the OBSERVED POSITION.
f) The Observed Position is marked by a circle with a dot in the centre ⊙ Another name for the Observed Position is a 'fix'.
g) The fix is the ACTUAL position of the ship.
h) The arrow head indicating the Position Line always points AWAY from the mark (i.e. always towards the observer).
i) A RUNNING FIX may be used to find a position. In this method only one landmark need be used. This involves knowing the direction of the boat's track, the boat's speed, and transferring a position line.
k) A transferred position line has two arrowheads at each end, pointing outwards and is always parallel to the position line from which you transfer it.

Now do Exercise 4

'Glad we got a reliable fix before the fog came down. It's a relief to know we've cleared that rock'.

Exercise 4

This exercise is all about Position Lines and Observed Positions. When plotting your fix remember to
1. Mark an arrow head pointing towards you
2. Write in the time of the plot
3. Record the fix as a circle with a dot in it.
   (There is no need to draw the complete Position Line; just where it intersects with another will do).
4. Whenever a bearing of a headland is given always use the shoreline as the mark unless stated otherwise.

a) A ship is heading on a course of 180° and a bearing of 145° is taken of a headland. Will the headland lie to port or starboard of the ship?
b) A vessel anchors in an estuary and the skipper takes bearings as follows:

   Light house 123°   Chimney 210°   Church 344°

   Several hours later the boat has swung to the tide and points in the opposite direction. Will the bearings alter?
c) At 1234 the following bearings were taken:

   RHE* Gribbin Head 112°   Killyvarder Rock 043°

   What is the 1234 fix?
d) At 1455 an extract from a ship's log reads as follows:

   LHE Nare Head 270°   RHE Dodman Point 064°

   1) What is the 1455 fix?
   2) Do you consider this to be a reliable plot?
e) On 21 July 1975 at 1100 the skipper of a yacht sailing in Veryan Bay takes the following bearings:
   Hill 95 metres
   (just to the westerly of St Michael's Church Caerhays)   321°
   RHE Dodman Point   083°
   Caerhays Castle   354°
   What is the 1100 Obs. Pos. (Observed Position)?
f) On 22 July 1975 at 0100 a boat situated to the south west of the Eddystone lighthouse is sailing on a track of 100° at a constant speed of 6 knots, with the lighthouse bearing 040°. Twenty minutes later (at 0120) the lighthouse bears 335°. What is her Observed Position at 0120?

Answers overleaf

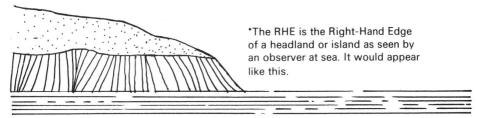

*The RHE is the Right-Hand Edge of a headland or island as seen by an observer at sea. It would appear like this.

Answers: Exercise 4

a) Port
b) No
c) 50°19'.5N   04°43'W
d) 1) 50°11'.7N   04°52'.2W   2) The angle of cut is too large to make for a reliable fix.
e) 1100 Obs. Pos. 50°13'N   04°50'.4W
f) This was a running fix taken in the hours of darkness.
  0120 Obs. Pos. 50°09'.1N   04°14'.6W

You should have got ALL the right answers. If you didn't, go over the incorrect part again, and again, and again.

Read on

UNIT 5 The Dead Reckoning Position

If a sailor knows his starting position (i.e. if he gets a fix) and the track his craft is making, then it is a simple enough job to deduce where he will end up, providing he knows the boat's speed. In other words an advance position may be plotted. Again, to make it easier to understand the principle, tides and winds have been disregarded.

Speed at sea is registered in KNOTS.

1 KNOT = 1 NAUTICAL MILE PER HOUR.

Move on to page 63

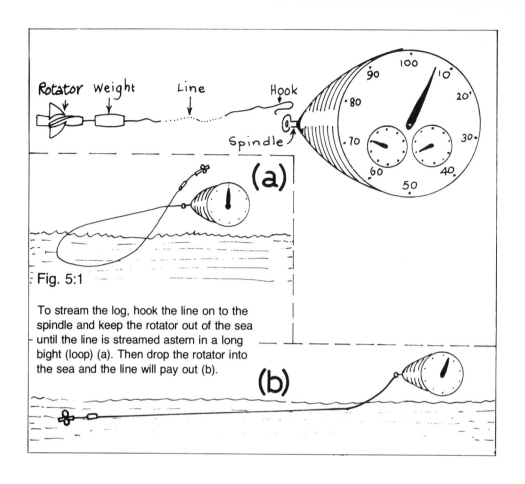

Fig. 5:1

To stream the log, hook the line on to the spindle and keep the rotator out of the sea until the line is streamed astern in a long bight (loop) (a). Then drop the rotator into the sea and the line will pay out (b).

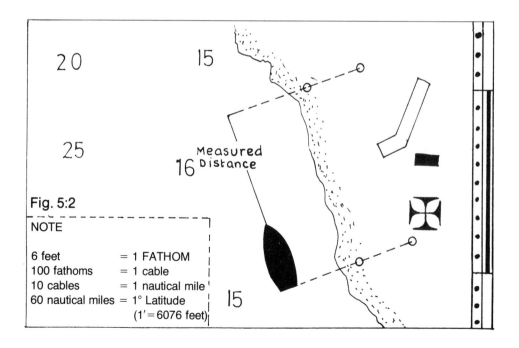

Fig. 5:2

NOTE

6 feet	= 1 FATHOM
100 fathoms	= 1 cable
10 cables	= 1 nautical mile
60 nautical miles	= 1° Latitude
	(1′ = 6076 feet)

There are three ways in which a vessel's speed may be found.

a) The use of some sort of instrument which will 'clock up' the number of miles the boat has travelled. A 'Walker Log' is a popular measuring device which consists of a rotator (a specially designed propeller) streamed astern of the vessel causing the log line to rotate and hence the mechanism attached to the vessel. A dial on the mechanism displays the distance travelled (fig. 5:1). An additional feature which may be fitted to the 'Walker Log' records the actual present speed which the boat is doing.

Another instrument used for recording speed and distance travelled employs the principle of a small paddled unit fitted to the hull which spins by the flow of the water. This movement activates electrical impulses which are translated into a meter reading. The speed and distance travelled is registered on a dial which looks something like a speedometer on a car.

b) By sailing between two known positions and noting the time taken during the 'run' the speed may be found. On many charts 'measured miles' are marked by the use of poles situated in transit (Fig. 5:2). Also look at the measured mile between Polperro and Looe (practice chart). For example, if a craft sailed over the mile in 10 minutes then her speed would be 6 knots.

1 mile in 6 minutes would be 10 knots
1 mile in 3 minutes would be 20 knots
1 mile in 12 minutes would be 5 knots

c) If the boat's speed or distance indicator fails, a good idea of speed through the water may be obtained by the 'Dutchman's Log'. Drop something which floats over the bow, and time its passage down the side of the hull between two points whose exact distance apart is known. Then:

$$\text{Speed in knots} = \frac{\text{Distance in feet}}{\text{Time in seconds}} \times \frac{3}{5}$$

Make sure that the object thrown overboard doesn't pollute the sea.

What would be the speed if the boat sailed 1 mile in $5\frac{1}{2}$ minutes:

10.9 knots . . . page 65
9.8 knots . . . page 67

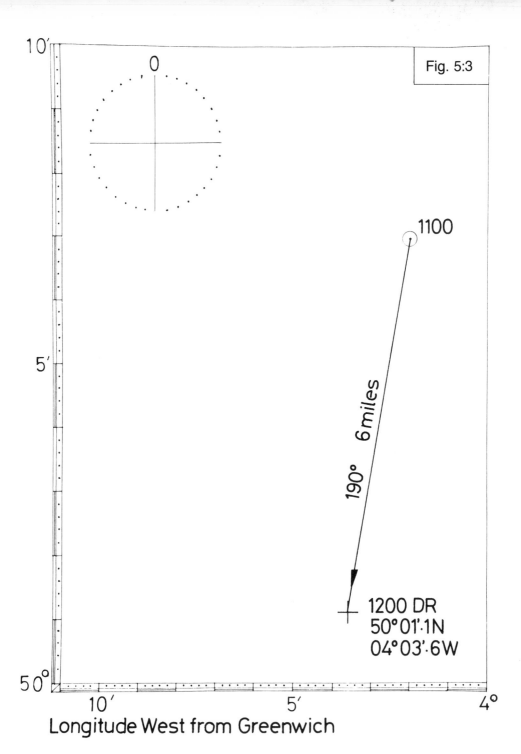

Fig. 5:3

0

1100

190° 6 miles

1200 DR
50°01'·1N
04°03'·6W

50°

10'

5'

4°

5'

10'

Longitude West from Greenwich

After a navigator has taken into account his starting position, the ship's track and her speed, he can then plot an advance position. This position is called the DEAD RECKONING POSITION. 'Dead' comes from 'deduced' – so Dead Reckoning Position really means Deduced Position.

This position, which is fundamental to all navigation, does not take account of TIDAL or WIND influences.

Take the following example: This has been worked out on the practice chart but an illustration of the plot is shown in Fig. 5:3.

> On 2 September 1973 at 1000 hours the skipper of a powered launch takes a reading of the log which turns out to be 6.7 miles. There is no wind or tidal stream influence. At 1100 the Observed Position is 50°07'N 04°02'W and the log reads 12.7 miles. The vessel's course is 190°. What is the Dead Reckoning (DR) Position at 1200?

The boat has travelled 6 miles in 1 hour (12.7–6.7), so her speed may be estimated as 6 knots.

First of all plot the Starting Position (fix), which is 50°07'N 04°02'W, and then the course which is 190°. Mark the course with one arrow head.

Along this course line measure 6 miles and at the end of the run draw a cross +*. This cross marks the DR Position at 1200 (answer opposite). The DR Position may be reckoned for time intervals of more or less than an hour. Do the next example using the practice chart.

At 1430 a launch in Obs. Pos. 50°02'N 04°10'W sets course 020°at an estimated speed of 5 knots. There is no wind or tide. What is the 1600 DR Pos.? In other words where do you deduce she will end up after 1½ hours' run?

1600 DR Pos. 50°09'N 03°14'W . . . *page 69*
1600 DR Pos. 50°06'.7N 04°07'.5W . . . *page 71*
1600 DR Pos. 50°09'N 04°06'W . . . *page 72*

---

*An alternative way of marking the DR Position is to put a small line at a right angles to the course line. Instead of putting ⊢➤ you may put ⤬➤

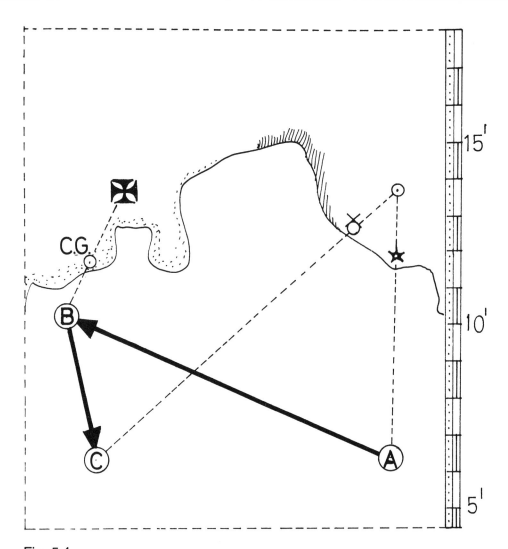

Fig. 5:4

Between A and B the boat sails 10 miles (77–67) in 2 hours.
Speed = Distance ÷ Time = $\dfrac{10}{2}$ = 5 knots.

Between B and C the boat sails 4 miles (81–77) in 15 minutes.
Speed = Distance ÷ Time = $\dfrac{4}{15} \times 60$ = 16 knots

X *You got the wrong answer.*

If you can read, add, subtract, multiply and divide then it is possible to do any normal navigational exercise. The answer 9.8 knots is wrong and it is likely that the fractions 'threw' you.

For example, had the question been 'What would be the speed if the craft took 1 hour (60 mins) to travel the mile?' you would easily have got the answer of 1 knot. Similarly, had the time to do the journey of 1 mile been 30 minutes instead of 1 hour, you would have seen that the speed would have doubled to 2 knots.

If you prefer to have a formula to work by,

DISTANCE = TIME × SPEED

From this we get
   TIME = DISTANCE ÷ SPEED
   SPEED = DISTANCE ÷ TIME

To apply the method to the original question on page 63:

SPEED = DISTANCE ÷ TIME   SPEED = 1 mile ÷ $5\frac{1}{2}$ minutes

Therefore SPEED = .181, and this would be the distance travelled in nautical miles in 1 minute. If we want to find the nautical miles travelled in 1 hour then we must multiply .181 by 60 (the number of minutes in 1 hour).

.181 × 60 = 10.86 (10.9) knots.

Referring to Fig. 5:4, a boat sails between certain known positions. At 'A' the log reads 67, at 'B' it reads 77 and at 'C' 81. The boat takes 2 hours to go from 'A' to 'B' and 15 minutes to travel from 'B' to 'C'. What speeds does the craft make during the passage? Consult the calculations opposite and then move back to page 63.

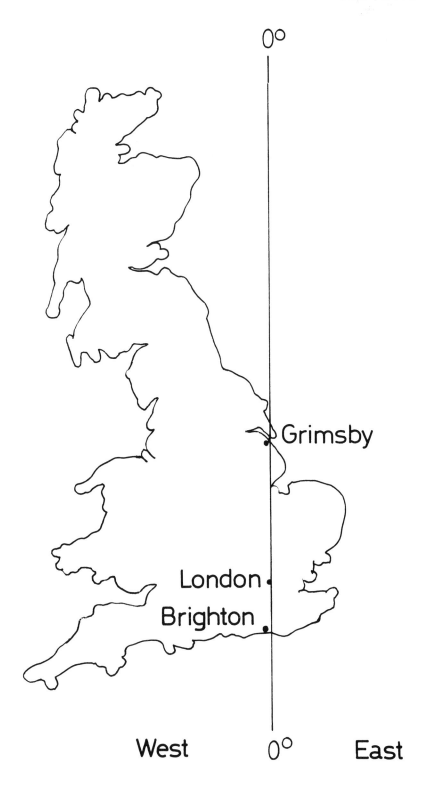

0°

West   0°   East

Grimsby

London

Brighton

Wrong, your Latitude plot is correct but you have read the Longitude from 'left to right', that is going east instead of west. The correct Longitude is 04°06'W. If you recall, in Unit 1 you learned to look at the bottom of the chart in order to confirm whether the Longitude was West or East. It is always wise to check this if you have any feeling of doubt.

However, unless your sailing area is in the vicinity of the Greenwich Meridian, somewhere like Brighton or Grimsby for example, then it is usual to find yourself in a well-defined East or West region. Weekend sailors who operate on, say, the Welsh coast, would 'live' with a westerly Longitude and they would probably have few occasions to cross the Greenwich Meridian.

Look at Fig. 5:5 and then return to page 65. Have another go at doing the problem which you got wrong.

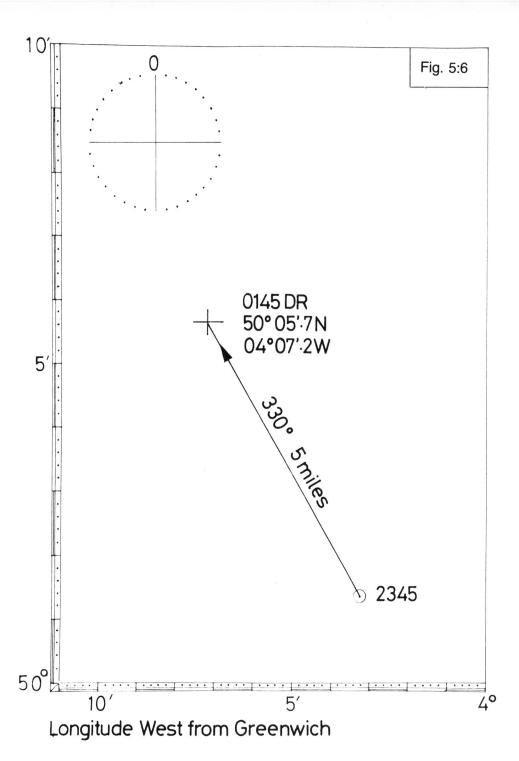

0

Fig. 5:6

0145 DR
50° 05'·7N
04° 07'·2W

330° 5 miles

2345

10'

5'

50°

10'

5'

4°

Longitude West from Greenwich

It is often the practice in coastal navigation to work by the hour but this is by no means always the case; to do so would be quite unnecessary during the course of many passages.

The mistake you made was to presume that the boat travelled over an hour's run, whereas she sailed at a speed of 5 knots for $1\frac{1}{2}$ hours (i.e. from 1430 hours to 1600 hours). Her distance covered in that period of time would therefore have been $7\frac{1}{2}$ miles (5 miles in 1 hour and $2\frac{1}{2}$ miles in $\frac{1}{2}$ hour).

Consider this next problem:

At 2345 a vessel in Obs. Pos. 50°01'.4N 04°03'.3W sets course 330°. Assuming the speed remains a steady $2\frac{1}{2}$ knots for 2 hours, what is the DR Position at 0145?

On the adjoining chart the initial position has been plotted and the track drawn in. Since the period in question is 2 hours, the distance run will be 5 miles ($2\frac{1}{2}$ × 2). The DR Position is therefore 50°05'.7N 04°07'.2W.

You should check the plot opposite and see if you agree.

Here's another, slightly different, problem:

A skipper takes a fix and establishes his position at 1230 as 50°02'.5N 04°07'W. The estimated speed of the boat is about 3 knots. After sailing due north for half an hour an alteration of course is made to 300°. After yet another half hour's run the original course is set (due north). Is 50°06'.2N 04°09'W the 1400 DR Position? If you think the answer is No please move to page 65.

Move to page 72

Well done. To get this far you must have understood the method of plotting the Dead Reckoning Position. After you have read the following summary, do the questions in Exercise 5 on page 73.

Summary

a) Given an Observed Position, the ship's speed and the course, the Dead Reckoning Position may be plotted by simply measuring along the course line the distance travelled in a certain known period of time.

b) It is sometimes useful to plot an hour's run but there is no hard and fast rule about this.

c) The DR position is marked by a cross +.

d) In plotting the DR Position no account is taken of winds and tides.

e) The DR Position is fundamental to all navigational procedures.

f) Since it is essential to know where you will end up it follows that the DR Position is a position which is ALWAYS PLOTTED IN ADVANCE.

Move to the next page

Exercise 5 *(refer to practice chart)*

(In this exercise there is no wind or tide implied)
a) At 1200 a boat is in a position 50°10′.5N   04°53′W, heading on a course of 130°. Her estimated speed is 4 knots. What is the 1300 DR Position?
b) At 2345 a vessel is in position 50°01′N   04°55′W and heading for St Anthony Head Light House. Her speed is 3 knots.
   1. What is the 0115 DR Position?
   2. What is the Estimated Time of Arrival (ETA) at the light house?
c) At 1800 auxiliary yacht *Griffin* leaves Looe Harbour (assume from the pier head light) and sets course 143°. If the estimated speed is 4½ knots, what is the 1900 DR Position?
d) At 1100 a vessel's log read 80½ miles. Her noon position is 50°10′N 04°41′W and she is bound 190°, her log reading 85. If she maintains her speed what is the 1300 DR Position?
e) At 0715 a sloop departs from the eastern end of Plymouth Breakwater and steers course 211°. Her estimated speed is 5 knots. What is the 0815 DR Position?

(Remember you should achieve accuracy to within 0.1′ (distances and position plots) and 1° (courses).)

Answers on next page

Answers: Exercise 5

a) 1300 DR Pos. 50°07'.9N   04°48'.3W.

b) 1.   1½ hour's run is 4½ miles. Course 333°. 0115 DR Pos. is 50°05'N 04°58'.2W.

2. 8.35 miles to run at 3 knots. Using formula Time = Distance ÷ Speed we get 8.35 ÷ 3 = 2.78 hours, which is about 2 hours 47 minutes. The ETA is 2345 + 2 hours 47 minutes = 0232 next day.

c) 1900 DR Pos. 50°17'.4N   04°22'.8W

d) Distance covered 1100 to 1200 is 4½ miles, therefore speed is 4½ knots. 1300 DR Pos. 50°05'.6N   04°42'.2W.

e) 0815 DR Pos. 50°15'.7N   04°12'.2W.

It is possible that any discrepancy between these answers and yours is due to your using a section of the Latitude scale which is remote from the area of activity. It may be worth your while to check this factor first if errors do occur.

If, after a double check, the number of correct answers falls below 4, you should do the unit again and re-think the problems. A complete understanding of the Dead Reckoning is essential at this stage.

Carry on to Unit 6

UNIT 6 Leeway

From a known position (fix) the boat will travel along her course line and end up at the DR Position provided there are no influences such as winds or tides which may affect her progress. We have discussed the method of plotting the DR Position and its significance – that of being a future position.

If there were no winds or tides then our boat's track would be in the same direction as her course. But there are winds and tides and they do play an important part in the way we forecast the future position.

What we are going to do in this unit is to look at the way WIND can alter our progress and we shall see how this force often shapes the ship's track which is not then the initial course steered. The method is to start from a determined fix and plot the track we shall make good. In this way we can forecast another future position which is called the ESTIMATED POSITION.

Move to page 77 please

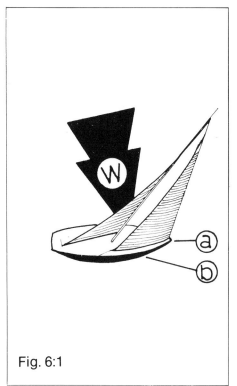

Fig. 6:1

Fig. 6:2

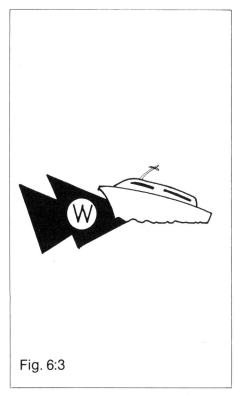

Fig. 6:3

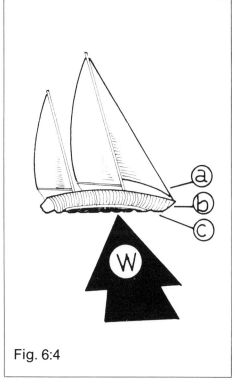

Fig. 6:4

Owing to the effect of the wind a boat tends to travel sideways as well as forwards. The end result is that she will be taken down wind of her course line. She is said to make LEEWAY.

Look at Fig. 6:1 and you will see that the yacht is heading on a course which is marked as 'a', but since the wind is blowing on her port side then her actual track made good will be 'b'.

If the wind is coming from astern (following) then there is no leeway (Fig. 6:2).

Yachts are usually more prone to leeway than are powered vessels and this applies very much in a situation where there is a sluggish yacht as compared with a high-powered motor cruiser. In Fig. 6:3 a powered craft is illustrated, but in any event there is no leeway because the wind is head-on and, like the instance of the following wind, there is no sideways effect.

In Fig. 6:4 which of the two positions 'a' or 'c' would the yacht finish up in?

'a' . . . *page 81*
'c' . . . page 79

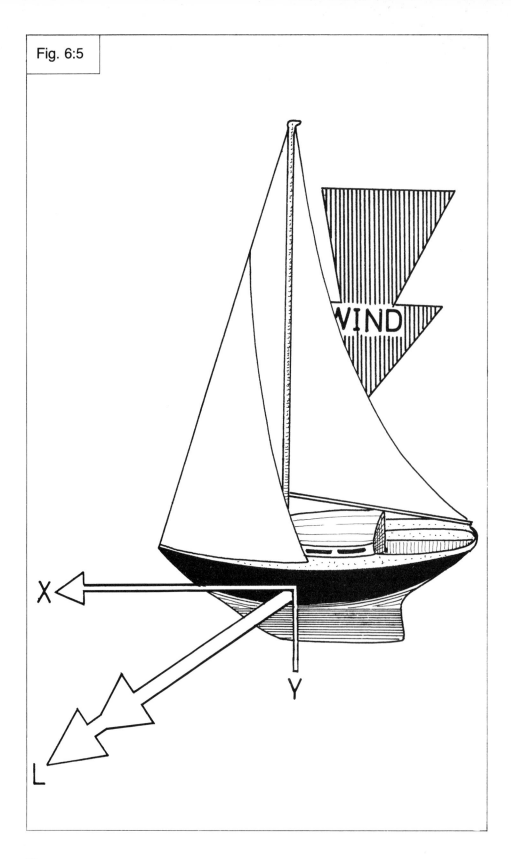

$\boxed{X}$ *Not correct*

'C' would have been the right position if the yacht had been on the other tack (the wind coming from the other side).

As it is she is sailing with the wind on her starboard side; her ultimate position may be estimated to be somewhere to the leeward (down wind) and this would set her at position 'a'.

Look at Fig. 6:5. The arrow pointing along the direction of the boat's head ('X') is the course steered. Line 'Y' is the actual sideways component which is caused by the wind hitting the vessel from the side.

Together these two components, the forward way 'X' and the sideways way 'Y', produce a result 'L' (track made good).

It may help to envisage the direction of the line 'Y' when working out on which side of the course line 'X' a ship will end up.

Page 81

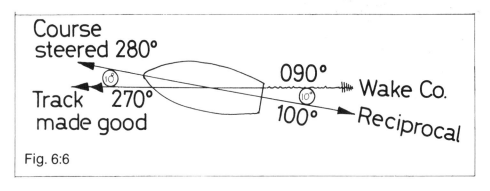

Course steered 280°

Track made good 270°

10°

090° Wake Co.

100° Reciprocal

10°

Fig. 6:6

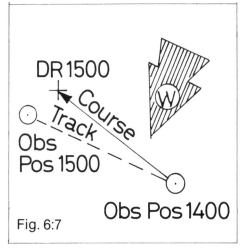

DR 1500

Obs Pos 1500

Course

Track

Obs Pos 1400

Fig. 6:7

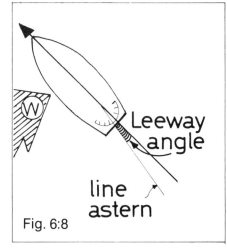

W

Leeway angle

line astern

Fig. 6:8

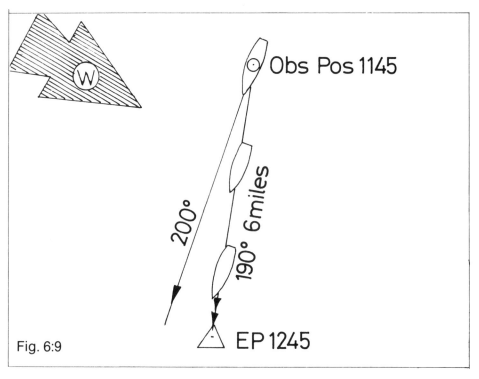

W

Obs Pos 1145

200°

190° 6miles

EP 1245

Fig. 6:9

$\boxed{V}$ *Good*

Assuming that there is no tidal stream then leeway may be defined as THE ANGLE BETWEEN THE COURSE STEERED AND THE TRACK MADE GOOD. Here are some ways of finding the leeway:

a) Compare a bearing of the 'wake' course of the boat and the reciprocal of the course steered. The wake (sea-track showing astern of the vessel) is often clearly seen as a boat moves through the water, particularly if she is moving quickly. In Fig. 6:6 the reciprocal of the course of 280° is 100° (280°–180°), so the angle of leeway is 10° (100°–090°).

b) A comparison between DR Position and the Observed Position should give the angle of leeway, again providing there are no tidal influences. Fig. 6:7 shows the course line with the DR marked on it and the boat's track (dotted line). The angle between the two is the leeway because the wind is responsible for the difference.

c) Another method is to trail a line astern (some people use a log line). The angle which this line makes with the 'fore and aft' line of the boat is the leeway. Some sailors mount a protractor on the stern in order to read off the leeway angle. Look at Fig. 6:8.

However, it should be emphasised that leeway is not simply and easily found under all sea conditions. Most sailors would agree that leeway is estimated only after a skipper gets to 'know' his craft.

Leeway, when applied to the course line, enables us to work out where we think we shall end up, providing we know the speed. In Fig. 6:9 a boat in Observed Position 1145 sets course 200°. Her estimated speed, which was obtained by a comparison of log readings over the previous hour's run, is 6 knots. Leeway is estimated as 10°, wind NW force 4.* (Don't forget that this wind will blow FROM the north-west). The wind is therefore on the starboard side of the boat; she is said to be on the starboard tack. Leeway results in a vessel being taken bodily DOWN WIND of her course line. You are reminded that there exists no tidal stream for the purposes of this illustration. What we should do now is to ESTIMATE where the boat will be at say, 1245.

1. Plot the course line which is 200°.
2. Plot the track made good (often called the leeway track). This will be 190° (200°–10°). Measure along this track 6 miles.
3. The ESTIMATED POSITION (EP) is at the end of this 6 mile run and is marked with a triangle with a dot in the centre and written as EP 1245.

Do the next example on the practice chart.

At 2130 a boat in Obs. Pos. 50°08'N   04°51'W steers a course of 260° Her speed is 4 knots, wind NW 4 and leeway 5°. What is the 2230 EP?

50°07'N   04°57'·1W . . . *page 82*
Any other answers . . . *page 85*

---

*Having found the leeway angle it is not necessary to know the strength of the wind (e.g. force 4) to find the track made good. However, since it is customary for wind direction and strength to be recorded this form will continue to be followed in the programme.

☑ *Correct. Now read the following summary and then do Exercise 6.*

Summary

a) Because of the wind a boat travels sideways as well as forwards.
b) The end result is that she will be settled DOWNWIND of the course line.
c) Leeway is the angle between the course steered and the track made good (no tidal streams implied).
d) Leeway, when applied to the course, enables us to plot the track made good and then the ESTIMATED POSITION.
e) The EP is always marked as a triangle with a dot in the centre △ .

Exercise 6 is on the opposite page

Exercise 6

Remember to draw in the track made good DOWNWIND of the course line. Up to now you have been taught to plot the course line and then the leeway track. You will probably have realised that it is not necessary to plot the course line: you can plot the leeway track straight away. Plot the correct symbol △ for EP.

a) If a small boat steers a course of 265° and if her estimated leeway is 5° what is the track made good? (Wind SW force 4).

b) At 1645 a yacht which is heading 170° and maintaining a speed of $3\frac{1}{2}$ knots is at Obs. Pos. 50°11'N   04°49'W. There are no tidal streams and the wind is E force 4. At 1745 her Obs. Pos. is 50°07'.5N   04°48'.8W. What is her angle of leeway between 1645 and 1745?

c) At 2015 a skipper takes a fix which turns out to be 50°06'N   05°00'W. He sets course 100°. Wind NE force 3. If he continues on this course at a mean speed of 6 knots what would be the EP 2115? Leeway is estimated at 10°.

d) Complete this table (no tidal streams implied):

Course steered	Wind	Leeway	Track made good
280°	SW	15°	
001°	NE	10°	
045°	E		040°
190°	SE		198°
320°	N	10°	

e) At 1430 a yacht in Obs. Pos. 50°10'.5N   04°49'W steers a course of 137°. The wind is NE force 4, and leeway estimated at 8°. If there are no tidal streams to contend with and if the estimated speed is 4 knots, what will be:

1. Track made good?
2. 1530 EP?

Answers on page 86

Fig. 6:10

Plot the 0245 fix

0245 ⊙

Plot the boat's course

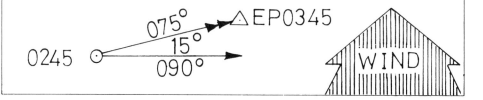

0245 ⊙————————090°————————▶

Plot the track made good. The way to do this is to relate the wind direction to the heading of the craft. In this instance the wind is on the starboard side of the vessel. The leeway track will be 075° (090°–15°). Plot the 0345 EP 4 miles from the 0245 fix.

075°   △EP0345
15°
0245 ⊙————————090°————————▶

WIND

Fig. 6:11

In the following example do you think the wind is coming from the north or south? Before you decide imagine yourself actually on the boat and define the direction in which she is being swept off her course. (The answer is at the bottom of this illustration.)

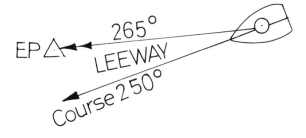

EP △◀————265°————
LEEWAY
Course 250°

The wind direction is the same as it is in Fig. 6:10

84

$\boxed{X}$ *This time you got it wrong.*

If you meet the problem of deciding what the track made good is in relation to the course steered, draw a diagram and work it out logically. Take the following example:

A yacht in Obs. Pos. 0245 is heading on a course of 090°. The wind is south and estimated leeway 15°. The boat's distance run between 0245 and 0345 is 4 miles. What is the Estimated Position at 0345?

a) Plot the 0245 fix.
b) Plot the course line.
c) Plot the track made good by drawing a line 15° to the course line. In this case the 15° should be subtracted from the course because the wind is hitting the starboard side of the boat and the track made good is down wind of the course line.
d) Plot the EP at 0345 (4 miles from the 0245 fix on the track made good).

Refer to Fig. 6:10 where the problem is illustrated.

After you have looked at 6:10 study Fig. 6:11 and then move back to page 82

Answers: Exercise 6

a) She is on the port tack so track made good is 265° + 5° = 270°.
b) Track made good is 178° (join up the two Observed Positions). Leeway is the difference between course steered (170°) and the track made good (178°) i.e. 8°.
c) 2115 EP 50°04'N   04°51'.2W.
d)

Course steered	Wind	Leeway	Track Made Good
280°	SW	15°	295°
001°	NE	10°	351°
045°	E	5°	040°
190°	SE	8°	198°
320°	N	10°	310°

e) 1.   Track made good 145°
   2.   1530 EP 50°07'.2N   04°45'.4W

Carry on to Test Piece B which is on the next page

Test Piece B

The following piece is arranged as a continuing problem. However, you would be wise to check each separate answer. Don't forget that if you get a 'cocked hat' it is wise to assume that you are at the centre or at the corner nearest to any danger.

a) At 1810 a yacht is sailing in Gerrans Bay. The navigator takes the following bearings:

    Hill 77 metres (near Pendower) 295°
    Carne Beacon 039°

    What is the 1810 fix?

b) At 1810 a course of 138° is set to run out of the bay. The wind is NW force 3 and there are no tidal streams. The log reads 8.8 and the estimated speed of the craft is 5 knots. What is the 1840 DR Position?

c) At 1840 the navigator observes the boat's position as 50°10′N 04°54′W. The log reads 11.3, there are still no tidal streams, and wind remains steady at NW force 3. Why do you think there is a difference between the 1840 DR Pos. and the 1840 Obs. Pos.?

d) At 1840 a course of 040° is set and the speed increases to 6 knots. The wind is still at NW force 3. The leeway is 15°. What is the 1910 EP?

e) At 1910 the following bearings were taken. The log reads 15.

    LHE Nare Head 267°
    St Michael's Church, Caerhays 352°

    What is the 1910 Obs. Pos?

This piece should not have caused you too much trouble. Always remember to use the Observed Position as a starting position and then estimate the future DR Position and Estimated Position.

Answers overleaf

Answers: Test Piece B

a) 1810 fix 50°11'.8N   04°56'.5W.

b) In this case the DR Pos. is plotted for only half an hour's run. 1840 DR 50°09'.9N   04°53'.9W.

c) The difference is not caused through leeway because the boat is before the wind and there is no sideways effect on the yacht (see Fig. 6:2 page 76). Likely factors accounting for this discrepancy are probably miscalculation – bad fixes resulting from unreliable bearings and wrong estimated speed and distance run.

d) The 1840 fix becomes the starting point from which to lay off the course line 040°. The wind is NW so the boat is on the port tack (wind hitting the port side). The track made good is therefore downwind of 040° by 15°. The track made good is 055°.

   1910 EP is 50°11'.7N   04°50'.2W (half an hour's run is 3 miles).

e) 1910 fix 50°11'.9N   04°50'.7W

Read on

UNIT 7 Tidal Streams

We have previously deliberately avoided any precise reference to tidal influences.

We have seen how to plot the Observed Position, which becomes a 'starting point'. Then, in relation to the course steered and distance travelled, a future position was plotted (DR).

Because we knew that leeway would inevitably affect our progress we were able to account for this influence and use our information of it to plot a more accurate future position and this was labelled the EP.

In this unit we learn how to select information about tidal streams and in the next unit we learn how to apply it.

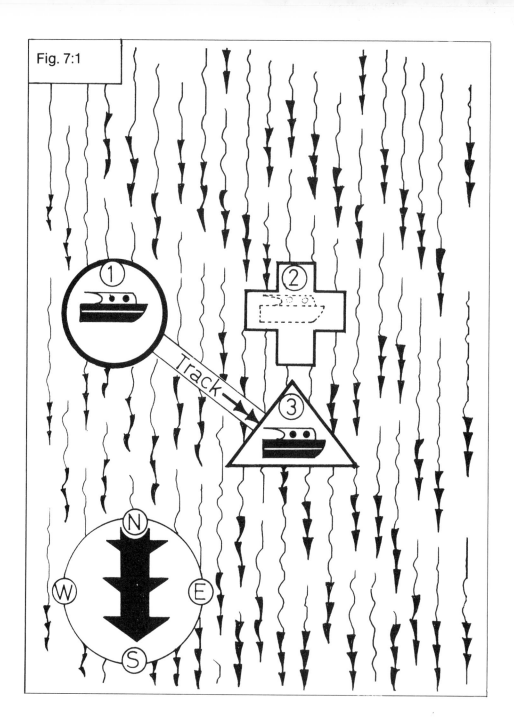

Fig. 7:1

In Fig. 7:1 a small powered vessel is heading on an easterly course. If there were no wind and no tidal stream then she would have made good a track which is also easterly, and reached position '2', which is of course the DR Position.

Now assume, however, there is a tidal stream setting to the south: because of this the craft is gradually moved off her original easterly track (not course!) and she would end up in position '3', which is both east and south of her original position '1'.

In this example a tidal stream which is setting to the south is shown and, unlike winds, streams set or travel TOWARDS their named direction. You will recall that winds always come FROM their named direction.

Thus a southerly tidal stream always sets TOWARDS the south (180°), northerly TOWARDS the north (000°), easterly TOWARDS the east (090°), and so on. Notice that tidal streams are marked by three arrow heads.

A boat, making headway and steering a course of 000°, encounters a tidal stream which is setting 045° while, at the same time, a fresh SW wind is blowing. Leeway is negligible. In which of the following positions will the craft end up?

A position north and east of the original position . . . *page 95*
A position south and east of the original . . . *page 93*

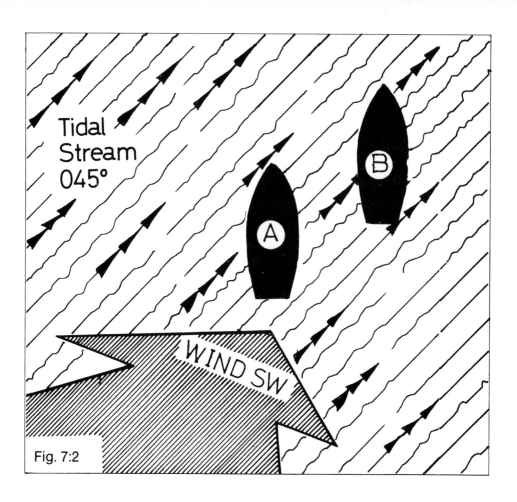

Tidal Stream 045°

A

B

WIND SW

Fig. 7:2

$\boxed{X}$ *Your answer is wrong.*

It can sometimes be very confusing that winds are said to come FROM while tidal streams are said to set TOWARDS.

If you look on the opposite page (Fig. 7:2) the situation under review is illustrated and it should be clear that both wind and tidal stream are moving in a NE direction.

The vessel must therefore reach a position which is to the north and east of her original one. She will go from 'A' to 'B' in fact.

Now turn to page 95

ENGLAND, SOUTH COAST — DEVONPORT
Lat. 50° 22′ N. Long. 4° 11′ W.

TIME ZONE: G.M.T.   TIMES AND HEIGHTS OF HIGH AND LOW WATERS   YEAR 1975

JULY

Day	Time	m	Ft.	Day	Time	m	Ft.
1 Tu	0408	1.7	5.5	16 W	0448	1.3	4.2
	1011	4.5	14.7		1107	4.8	15.6
	1623	1.9	6.3		1712	1.5	5.0
	2229	4.6	15.0		2329	4.8	15.7
2 W	0453	1.9	6.1	17 Th	0545	1.6	5.1
	1104	4.3	14.3		1206	4.6	15.2
	1716	2.1	6.9		1818	1.7	5.7
	2326	4.4	14.4				
3 Th	0552	2.0	6.6	18 F	0036	4.6	15.0
	1208	4.3	14.1		0655	1.8	5.9
	1824	2.2	7.2		1319	4.6	15.0
					1936	1.8	5.9
4 F	0033	4.3	14.1	19 Sa	0154	4.5	14.7
	0702	2.0	6.6		0810	1.7	5.6
	1318	4.3	14.2		1437	4.7	15.3
	1939	2.1	6.9		2051	1.7	5.5
5 Sa	0145	4.4	14.3	20 Su	0310	4.5	14.9
	0811	1.9	6.2		0920	1.5	5.0
	1426	4.5	14.8		1544	4.8	15.9
	2046	1.9	6.2		2155	1.4	4.8
6 Su	0250	4.5	14.8	21 M	0414	4.7	15.4
	0912	1.6	5.4		1019	1.3	4.3
	1525	4.7	15.5		1640	5.0	16.5
	2143	1.6	5.3		2249	1.2	4.0
7 M	0349	4.7	15.5	22 Tu	0508	4.9	15.9
	1007	1.4	4.5		1110	1.1	3.7
	1618	5.0	16.3		1728	5.2	16.9
	2235	1.3	4.2		2336	1.0	3.4
8 Tu	0444	4.9	16.2	23 W	0554	5.0	16.3
	1059	1.1	3.6		1155	1.0	3.3
	1709	5.2	17.1		1810	5.2	17.2
	2325	1.0	3.2				
9 W	0538	5.1	16.8	24 Th	0018	0.9	3.1
	1148	0.9	2.9		0633	5.0	16.5
	1800	5.4	17.7		1234	0.9	3.1
					1845	5.3	17.3
10 Th	0014	0.7	2.4	25 F	0055	0.9	2.9
	0631	5.3	17.2		0706	5.1	16.6
	1235	0.7	2.3		1309	1.0	3.2
	1850	5.5	18.1		1915	5.3	17.3
11 F	0100	0.5	1.8	26 Sa	0128	0.9	3.0
	0723	5.3	17.5		0735	5.0	16.6
	1320	0.6	2.0		1341	1.0	3.4
	1939	5.6	18.4		1942	5.2	17.2
12 Sa	0145	0.5	1.5	27 Su	0159	1.0	3.3
	0810	5.3	17.5		0800	5.0	16.4
	1404	0.6	2.1		1409	1.2	3.8
	2024	5.6	18.4		2007	5.2	17.0
13 Su	0229	0.5	1.7	28 M	0227	1.1	3.7
	0855	5.3	17.3		0825	4.9	16.2
	1447	0.7	2.5		1438	1.3	4.3
	2107	5.5	18.0		2034	5.0	16.6
14 M	0313	0.7	2.3	29 Tu	0257	1.3	4.3
	0936	5.1	16.8		0854	4.8	15.8
	1531	1.0	3.1		1508	1.5	4.9
	2150	5.3	17.4		2105	4.9	15.9
15 Tu	0358	1.0	3.2	30 W	0328	1.5	5.0
	1019	4.9	16.2		0927	4.6	15.3
	1618	1.2	4.0		1542	1.7	5.7
	2236	5.0	16.6		2141	4.6	15.2
				31 Th	0406	1.8	5.8
					1009	4.5	14.7
					1625	2.0	6.5
					2228	4.4	14.4

AUGUST

Day	Time	m	Ft.	Day	Time	m	Ft.
1 F	0453	2.0	6.5	16 Sa	0006	4.4	14.3
	1105	4.3	14.2		0621	2.0	6.5
	1723	2.2	7.2		1248	4.5	14.6
	2331	4.2	13.9		1911	2.0	6.7
2 Sa	0558	2.1	6.9	17 Su	0133	4.3	13.9
	1217	4.3	14.0		0748	2.0	6.6
	1840	2.2	7.4		1416	4.5	14.8
					2036	1.9	6.2
3 Su	0049	4.2	13.8	18 M	0259	4.4	14.4
	0719	2.1	6.8		0904	1.8	5.8
	1336	4.4	14.4		1529	4.7	15.5
	2003	2.1	6.8		2141	1.6	5.3
4 M	0209	4.4	14.3	19 Tu	0402	4.6	15.2
	0837	1.9	6.1		1004	1.5	4.9
	1448	4.6	15.2		1623	5.0	16.3
	2114	1.7	5.7		2233	1.3	4.3
5 Tu	0320	4.6	15.2	20 W	0451	4.9	16.0
	0943	1.5	4.9		1052	1.2	4.0
	1551	4.9	16.2		1707	5.2	17.0
	2214	1.3	4.3		2316	1.1	3.5
6 W	0423	4.9	16.2	21 Th	0531	5.1	16.6
	1039	1.1	3.7		1133	1.0	3.4
	1648	5.3	17.3		1744	5.3	17.4
	2308	0.9	3.0		2355	0.9	3.0
7 Th	0521	5.2	17.2	22 F	0606	5.2	17.0
	1131	0.8	2.6		1210	0.9	3.1
	1743	5.6	18.2		1817	5.4	17.7
	2358	0.6	1.9				
8 F	0617	5.4	17.9	23 Sa	0029	0.9	2.9
	1219	0.5	1.7		0637	5.2	17.2
	1836	5.8	18.9		1242	0.9	3.0
					1847	5.4	17.7
9 Sa	0045	0.3	1.1	24 Su	0100	0.9	2.9
	0708	5.6	18.3		0705	5.2	17.2
	1305	0.4	1.3		1313	1.0	3.2
	1926	5.9	19.2		1914	5.4	17.6
10 Su	0130	0.3	0.9	25 M	0129	1.0	3.2
	0756	5.6	18.3		0731	5.2	17.0
	1348	0.4	1.3		1341	1.1	3.5
	2012	5.8	19.1		1941	5.3	17.3
11 M	0212	0.4	1.2	26 Tu	0157	1.1	3.6
	0838	5.5	18.0		0756	5.1	16.8
	1429	0.5	1.7		1409	1.2	3.9
	2054	5.6	18.5		2005	5.1	16.8
12 Tu	0253	0.6	2.0	27 W	0225	1.3	4.2
	0917	5.3	17.4		0820	5.0	16.4
	1511	0.8	2.6		1438	1.4	4.6
	2133	5.3	17.5		2029	4.9	16.1
13 W	0335	1.0	3.2	28 Th	0255	1.5	4.8
	0955	5.1	16.7		0846	4.8	15.8
	1554	1.2	3.8		1509	1.6	5.3
	2213	5.0	16.4		2056	4.7	15.4
14 Th	0419	1.4	4.5	29 F	0328	1.7	5.6
	1037	4.8	15.8		0919	4.6	15.2
	1644	1.6	5.1		1547	1.9	6.2
	2301	4.6	15.2		2134	4.5	14.7
15 F	0512	1.7	5.7	30 Sa	0410	1.9	6.4
	1132	4.6	15.1		1009	4.5	14.7
	1747	1.9	6.2		1637	2.1	7.0
					2235	4.3	14.1
				31 Su	0509	2.1	7.1
					1122	4.4	14.3
					1751	2.3	7.4

SEPTEMBER

Day	Time	m	Ft.	Day	Time	m	Ft.
1 M	0000	4.2	13.8	16 Tu	0239	4.3	14.2
	0633	2.2	7.3		0844	2.0	6.5
	1249	4.4	14.4		1503	4.7	15.4
	1926	2.2	7.1		2113	1.7	5.7
2 Tu	0134	4.4	14.3	17 W	0359	4.6	15.3
	0806	2.0	6.6		0940	1.6	5.4
	1414	4.7	15.3		1555	5.0	16.3
	2049	1.8	5.9		2208	1.4	4.6
3 W	0256	4.7	15.3	18 Th	0423	4.9	16.2
	0920	1.6	5.2		1026	1.4	4.4
	1536	5.0	16.5		1636	5.2	17.1
	2153	1.3	4.3		2248	1.2	3.8
4 Th	0404	5.1	16.6	19 F	0500	5.2	16.9
	1019	1.1	3.7		1105	1.1	3.7
	1628	5.4	17.8		1712	5.4	17.7
	2240	0.8	2.7		2325	1.0	3.3
5 F	0503	5.4	17.7	20 Sa	0533	5.3	17.4
	1111	0.7	2.4		1140	1.0	3.3
	1724	5.8	18.9		1745	5.5	18.0
	2339	0.5	1.5		2358	0.9	3.0
6 Sa	0557	5.7	18.5	21 Su	0605	5.4	17.7
	1159	0.4	1.4		1212	1.0	3.1
	1817	6.0	19.6		1816	5.5	18.1
7 Su	0025	0.3	0.9	22 M	0030	0.9	3.0
	0647	5.8	19.0		0634	5.4	17.7
	1244	0.3	0.9		1243	1.0	3.2
	1907	6.0	19.7		1847	5.5	17.9
8 M	0109	0.2	0.8	23 Tu	0100	1.0	3.2
	0733	5.8	19.0		0703	5.4	17.6
	1327	0.3	1.0		1313	1.0	3.4
	1952	5.9	19.4		1915	5.3	17.5
9 Tu	0150	0.4	1.3	24 W	0129	1.1	3.6
	0815	5.7	18.6		0729	5.3	17.3
	1408	0.5	1.6		1343	1.2	3.9
	2033	5.7	18.6		1940	5.2	16.9
10 W	0230	0.7	2.3	25 Th	0158	1.3	4.1
	0852	5.4	17.8		0753	5.1	16.9
	1448	0.8	2.7		1413	1.4	4.4
	2110	5.3	17.4		2001	5.0	16.3
11 Th	0309	1.1	3.5	26 F	0228	1.5	4.8
	0926	5.2	17.0		0815	5.0	16.4
	1530	1.2	4.1		1444	1.6	5.1
	2147	4.9	16.2		2023	4.8	15.7
12 F	0351	1.5	4.9	27 Sa	0301	1.7	5.5
	1005	4.9	16.0		0844	4.8	15.9
	1617	1.7	5.5		1521	1.8	5.9
	2231	4.5	14.9		2059	4.6	15.1
13 Sa	0441	1.9	6.3	28 Su	0341	1.9	6.3
	1058	4.6	15.1		0932	4.7	15.4
	1718	2.1	6.8		1610	2.0	6.7
	2336	4.3	14.0		2201	4.4	14.5
14 Su	0550	2.2	7.2	29 M	0438	2.1	7.0
	1214	4.4	14.5		1043	4.5	14.9
	1845	2.2	7.3		1721	2.2	7.2
					2328	4.3	14.2
15 M	0109	4.2	13.7	30 Tu	0602	2.3	7.4
	0724	2.2	7.4		1212	4.6	15.0
	1348	4.5	14.6		1856	2.1	7.0
	2016	2.1	6.8				

Fig. 7:3

(Page from the Admiralty Tide Tables, Vo. 1, 1975, Part 1. Crown copyright. Reproduced with the permission of The Hydrographer of the Navy)

Well done, you reasoned that out very soundly.

Having understood that tidal streams are forces to be accounted for, what we have to do now is to find out WHEN and WHERE they are moving. Let's take the WHEN first.

All tidal calculations are normally referred to the time at which High Water takes place.

There are several sources where times of tidal movements may be found: Reed's Nautical Almanac, the Admiralty Tide Tables or even small booklets giving local tidal information which you can get from local booksellers. The Admiralty Tide Tables (A.T.T.) is a very comprehensive volume and this is the reference we shall use. The reason for this choice is because you will gain more of an insight into principles discussed than if you were to use more 'instant' methods.

On the opposite page is a sample of the A.T.T. (Fig. 7:3), and this illustrates information for Devonport which is the standard port of reference on our main practice chart.

Consider 1 July Devonport:

Date and day	Time	Height (metres)	Height (feet)
1 Tu	0408	1.7	5.5
	1011	4.5	14.7
	1623	1.9	6.3
	2229	4.6	15.0

For each day there are two High Water times and heights (1011 4.5m and 2229 4.6m). Similarly there are two Low Water times and heights (0408 1.7m and 1623 1.9m).*

However, in this unit we are only concerned with the times of High Water (HW). At the top of the A.T.T. pages the TIME ZONE is given and in the case of Fig. 7:3 this is G.M.T., which means Greenwich Mean Time. During the summer months the clock is put forward an hour to give us British Summer Time (B.S.T.), which prevails between March and October. Because our sample relates to the month of July we must add 1 hour to G.M.T. to get B.S.T.

So on 1 July 1975 our Devonport HW times now read 1111 B.S.T. (1011 G.M.T. + 1 hour) and 2329 B.S.T. (2229 G.M.T. + 1 hour).

What is the HW time (B.S.T.) at Devonport during the morning of 8 July? (Remember to add an hour to get B.S.T.)

0734 B.S.T. . . . *page 97*
0321 B.S.T. . . . *page 97*
Any other answer . . . *page 97*

---

*On some days only three times are given. This is because the time may 'overlap' into the next day. For example 9 July HW time is 1800 and the next LW time would be just into the next day at 0014 (0.7m).

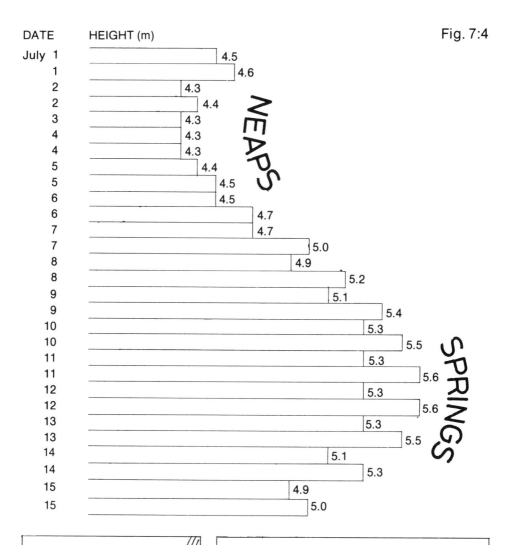

DATE HEIGHT (m) Fig. 7:4

DATE	HEIGHT (m)
July 1	4.5
1	4.6
2	4.3
2	4.4
3	4.3
4	4.3
4	4.3
5	4.4
5	4.5
6	4.5
6	4.7
7	4.7
7	5.0
8	4.9
8	5.2
9	5.1
9	5.4
10	5.3
10	5.5
11	5.3
11	5.6
12	5.3
12	5.6
13	5.3
13	5.5
14	5.1
14	5.3
15	4.9
15	5.0

NEAPS

SPRINGS

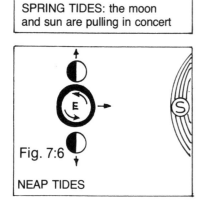

Fig. 7:5

SPRING TIDES: the moon and sun are pulling in concert

Fig. 7:6

NEAP TIDES

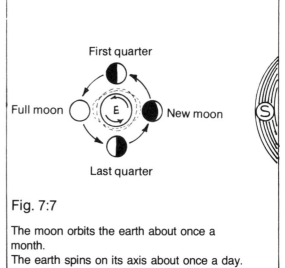

First quarter

Full moon   New moon

Last quarter

Fig. 7:7

The moon orbits the earth about once a month.
The earth spins on its axis about once a day.

The correct answer was 0544 B.S.T. (0444 G.M.T. + 1 hour). This is the first time that the correct answer to a question has not been included in the choice you had. There may be one or two more similar instances given to you in future pages.

Another close look at the HW times reveals that a significant variation of levels occurs. In other words the HW tide mark on a harbour wall on any one day will probably not be at the same level as the HW marks immediately before or after it.

Fig. 7:4 illustrates graphically the variations that occur during the month of July at Devonport. (The HW heights are taken from Fig. 7:3 on page 94). The heights start at 4.5m (1011 G.M.T.) on 1 July. The pattern which emerges shows a general downward trend which reaches a low point at about 3 and 4 July. After this heights start to climb until a peak is reached at about 11 and 12 July. After this date another downward trend emerges, and so on.

When the tides are at the 'peak' they are said to be SPRING tides, and they are called NEAP tides when they tend toward the 'valleys'. A glance at any tide tables will show that tides do build up (make) until they are at Springs, and then they fall away (take off) until they are again at Neaps; and this pattern repeats. Fig. 7:5, 7:6 and 7:7 explain why this is so. In Fig. 7:5 the moon is shown in two positions, both of which are in line with the earth and the sun. The combinations of the gravitational forces caused by the moon and sun in these positions bring about a build-up of water so that the seas of the earth (which should be imagined as covering it completely) are higher or heaped up in the areas nearest and furthest away from the moon. These are Spring tides.

The sun, for all its size, exerts relatively less gravitational force on the earth's oceans than the moon because it is further away. The moon then is the key where tides are concerned, and it is when this body is in either of the positions illustrated in Fig. 7:5 that Spring tides occur.

Fig. 7:6 depicts what happens when the moon and sun are not 'pulling' in concert. The 'heap' of water is somewhat flattened because to some extent the sun and moon are exerting forces in different directions. These are the Neap tides.

Now look again at Fig. 7:4 and attempt to answer the following question:

On July 7 the tides are

Springs . . . *page 99*
Midway between Springs and Neaps . . . *page 101*

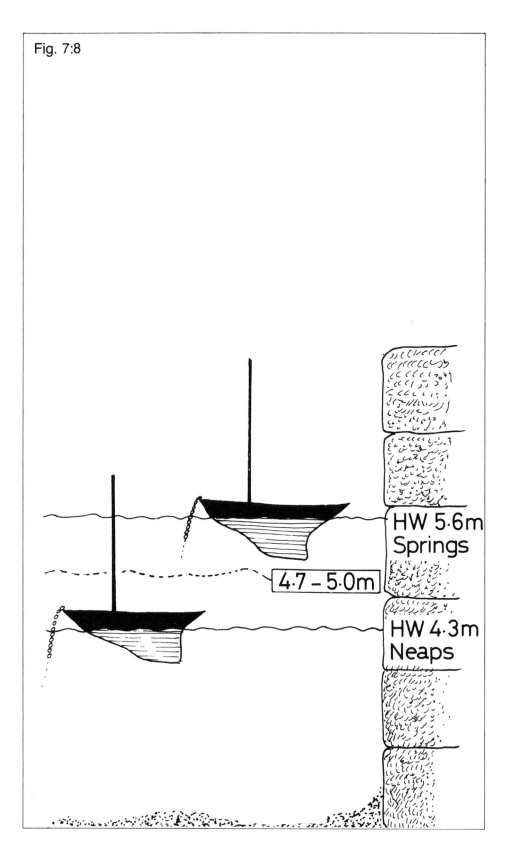

Fig. 7:8

HW 5·6m
Springs

4·7 – 5·0m

HW 4·3m
Neaps

'Springs' is incorrect. A look at Fig. 7:8 may help to clear up matters.

The two respective High Waters at Springs and Neaps are marked on the harbour wall. On 3 July the Neap HW height is 4.3m and this marks about the lowest the HW height will fall during the period proximate to 7 July, the day in question. The tidal level will increase until it reaches about 5.6m on 11 July.

The diagram shows that the yachts at anchor in the harbour would be floating at different heights according to whether they were at Springs or Neaps.

Clearly the 7 July level (height) of about 4.7 to 5.0m is approximately midway between 4.3m and 5.6m, so the tides at this date would be midway between Spring and Neaps.

Please continue

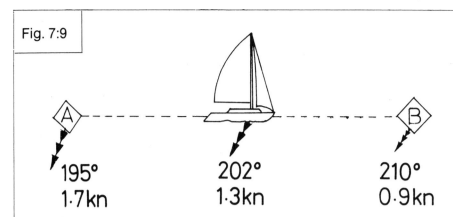

Fig. 7:9

195° 1·7kn   202° 1·3kn   210° 0·9kn

Hours	Ⓐ 50° 02'.4N 05° 02'.3W Rate (kn) Dir	Sp	Np	Ⓑ 50° 02'.5N 04° 58'.7W Rate (kn) Dir	Sp	Np
6	201	1.0	0.5	215	1.0	0.5
5	309	0.1	0.0	220	0.5	0.2
4	006	1.0	0.5	293	0.1	0.1
3	011	1.4	0.7	017	0.5	0.2
2	015	1.5	0.8	029	0.9	0.5
1	022	1.5	0.7	043	1.2	0.6
HW	028	1.2	0.6	043	1.2	0.6
1	030	0.5	0.2	040	0.7	0.4
2	202	0.4	0.2	slack		
3	196	1.2	0.6	214	0.5	0.3
4	195	1.7	0.9	210	0.9	0.5
5	197	1.6	0.8	213	1.3	0.6
6	202	1.2	0.6	216	1.2	0.6

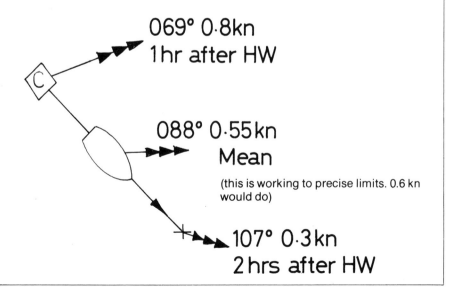

069° 0·8kn
1hr after HW

088° 0·55kn
Mean

(this is working to precise limits. 0.6 kn would do)

107° 0·3kn
2 hrs after HW

Now to find out WHERE the tidal streams are moving.

You will see that just underneath the practice chart heading there are tables called 'Tidal streams referred to HW Devonport', and these tables have sections each of which is related to a tidal diamond such as Ⓐ or Ⓑ. You should be familiar with Ⓓ because this was used in previous exercises. These tidal diamonds are places where tidal streams have been analysed over a period. The AVERAGE results are given in the table.

In order to find out in which direction the tidal streams are setting and at what time this is happening we must again find out when HW is. Look at the following example.

> At 1230 B.S.T. on 11 July 1975 a craft was on passage near the area of Ⓐ. What would be the predicted tidal stream in that area at that time?

In order to find out the answer you will need to know:
a) What is HW Devonport time nearest to 1230 (don't forget that we are working in B.S.T.)?
b) How many hours before or after HW time is 1230?
c) Are the tides Springs or Neaps?

Well, HW time nearest to 1230 is 0723 G.M.T. (0823 B.S.T.). You get this from page 94. 1230 is therefore 4 hours AFTER HW Devonport. The tides are at Springs (again look at page 94).

By glancing at the section labelled Ⓐ (which is re-written from the chart and included in Fig. 7:9) you can see that 4 hours after HW the direction is 195° and the Spring rate is 1.7 knots.

Similarly we can say that at the same time but at Ⓑ the direction is 210° at a Spring rate of 0.9 knots.

If you wanted to work out what the direction and rate of the expected tidal stream would be at the same time, 1230, but in between the two diamonds Ⓐ and Ⓑ, then you would have to do some intelligent guessing.

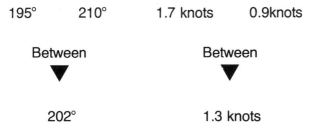

195°	210°	1.7 knots	0.9knots
Between		Between	
▼		▼	
202°		1.3 knots	

(refer to top drawing, Fig. 7:9)

However, what we have done so far on this page is to work out where the tidal streams were setting at a PARTICULAR MOMENT in time. But more realistically we can say that a sailor is more concerned with the problem of what the tidal streams are doing over a period of time such as 1 or more hours. Take the example overleaf, referring to the practice chart:

11 July 1975. At 0920 a yacht is in position ◇C sailing SE at 3 knots. There is no leeway. What tidal streams will she experience in the period 0920-1020?

First of all plot the course line and distance run between 0920 and 1020, using ◇ as the departure position. You will see that the boat is predominantly affected by the streams at ◇C . So what we want is the MEAN (average) of the tidal streams at ◇C between 0920 and 1020. Well, HW time is 0823, so we want to find the mean tidal stream between 1 hour after and 2 hours after H.W. Please look at the bottom of Fig. 7:9 and after you have done that 'try your hand' at doing the following.

4 July 1975. At 1215 a boat is at 50°08′N 04°51′W, under power on course 090°. Her estimated speed is 4 knots. There is no wind. What tidal streams would she expect in the period 1215-1315? (Answers upside down at the foot of the page.)

Summary

a) Tidal streams set TOWARDS their referred direction.
b) The Admiralty Tide Tables can be used to find out the times and heights of tides. Other publications contain similar information but the A.T.T. is used here.
c) All tidal stream calculations are based on the time of HW.
d) Tidal stream data is also printed on charts (tidal diamonds).
e) Tidal streams, when plotted, should be marked by three arrow heads.
f) AT BEST ALL TIDAL INFORMATION IS ESTIMATED AND SHOULD ALWAYS BE ACCEPTED AS APPROXIMATE.

Please do Exercise 7

Answers: HW on 4 July 1975 is 1318 G.M.T. (1418 B.S.T.). 1215 is 2 hours before HW, so tidal streams between 1215 and 1315 will be the mean between 2 hours before and 1 hour before HW. At ◇E the stream 2 hours before HW is 037° at 0.2 knots (Neaps) and 1 hour before HW is 042° at 0.3 knots. The mean tidal stream is 040° at 0.25 knots.

Exercise 7 (Throughout this exercise use B.S.T. and NOT G.M.T.)

a) Using the Tide Tables on page 94 complete the following table:

Date	Time of HW Devonport	Springs or Neaps?
2 July (pm) 12 July (pm) 14 July (pm) 20 July (am) 25 July (am) 27 July (am) 29 July (pm) 31 July (pm)		

b) Complete the following table of tidal stream calculations (refer to tidal information Ⓐ on the practice chart):

Time of HW Devonport	Time in question	Springs or Neaps	Direction and rate
1200	1100	Neaps	
1328	1030	Neaps	
2015	2320	Springs	
0010	0405	Springs	
0750	0320	Neaps	

c) A yacht is sailing in position 50°02′.5N   04°56′.6W at 1305 on Thursday 3 July 1975. What is the direction and rate of the tidal stream encountered?

d) A small boat is just off St Anthony Head sailing into Falmouth Harbour. The time is 1455. If HW Devonport on that day was 1000 would the craft be stemming (going against) or running with the tidal stream?

e) 12 July 1975. At 2130 a yacht is in position 50°17′N 04°27′W on course for the Eddystone Light. The wind is NW force 4 and leeway is negligible. The speed is 4 knots. What would be the expected tidal streams between 2130 and 2230?

f) At 1145 a boat, in position 50°10′N   04°50′W, drifts, becalmed and with faulty engine.

Assuming that the tidal stream information for the next three hours was thus,

1145–1245 093° at 0.8 knots
1245–1345 120° at 0.5 knots
1345–1445 181° at 0.4 knots
what would be her position at 1445?

Before you compare your answers with those on page 104 check to see that you have converted G.M.T. to B.S.T. (by adding 1 hour to G.M.T.).

Answers: Exercise 7

(a)

Date	Time of HW Devonport	Springs or Neaps?
2 July (pm)	1204	Neaps
12 July (pm)	2124	Springs
14 July (pm)	2250	Springs
20 July (am)	0410	Neaps
25 July (am)	0806	Springs
27 July (am)	0900	Springs
29 July (pm)	2205	Springs/Neaps
31 July (pm)	2328	Neaps

(b)

Time of HW Devonport	Time in question	Springs or Neaps	Direction and rate
1200	1100 (1 hr before)	Neaps	022° 0.7 knots
1328	1030 (3 hrs before)	Neaps	011° 0.7 knots
2015	2320 (3 hrs after)	Springs	196° 1.2 knots
0010	0405 (4 hrs after)	Springs	195° 1.7 knots
0750	0320 ($4\frac{1}{2}$ hrs before)	Neaps	about 338° at 0.25 knots

c) The boat is sailing about midway between tidal diamonds ⬦B and ⬦C . HW Devonport on 3 July is 1308, so it is about HW time when the boat is in this position. The tides are at Neaps and for ⬦B they would be 043° at 0.6 knots. At ⬦C they are 060° at 0.5 knots. The mean direction would be about 051° and the mean rate about 0.55 knots.

d) The time of sailing is about 5 hours after HW Devonport. At 5 hours after the direction of the tidal stream would be 180° (at diamond ⬦D). The craft would therefore be stemming the tide.

e) Our area of operations at 2130 and throughout the passage is ⬦F . HW on 12 July 1975 is 2024 G.M.T. (2124 B.S.T.), so the time in question, 2130, is about HW time. There are Spring tides. What we want is the mean tidal stream between HW and 1 hour after HW. At HW streams are 072° at a rate of 0.9 knots. At 1 hour after HW streams are 084° at a rate of 0.9 knots. Therefore mean tidal stream between 2130 and 2230 is 078° at a rate of 0.9 knots.

f) Plot the position at 1145. Then plot each of the three streams consecutively. She will be in position 50°09′.3N   04°48′.1W at 1445.

You should have got all the correct answers but in any event you should do the unit again if you failed to master questions (c), (d) or (e).

UNIT 8 Another Estimated Position

So you find out where you are (determine a fix) and set course. If there is no wind or tide then you would expect to arrive at the DR Position and you will recall that this position is plotted in advance.

In Unit 6 the effect of wind (leeway) was discussed and we learned how to plot another position called the Estimated Position (EP).

In the next few pages the knowledge gained about tidal streams will be applied so that we may estimate yet another position and this is again termed the ESTIMATED POSITION.

If the visibility is very good and there is plenty of sea room you may get by if you take frequent fixes and disregard any DR or EP. But in bad visibility, for example in fog or rain and certainly in the hours of darkness, you may find that the only position you have to fall back on is the EP. For this reason the EP is always plotted so that you have a good idea where you will end up. The whole procedure may be stated in just a few easy stages, like this:

First   Find the Observed Position. This is the 'starter'

Second   By using the course steered and distance run plot the DR Posi-
             tion. Remember that this is a FUTURE plot.

Third   Or if there is wind causing leeway plot the EP (to clarify we'll call
             this the 1st EP). Again this is a FUTURE plot.

Finally   By applying tidal stream direction and rate plot another EP (this
             we will call the final EP) – another FUTURE plot.

PLEASE REMEMBER THAT THIS PROCEDURE IS GEARED TO ESTIMATING A FUTURE POSITION.

Page 107 now

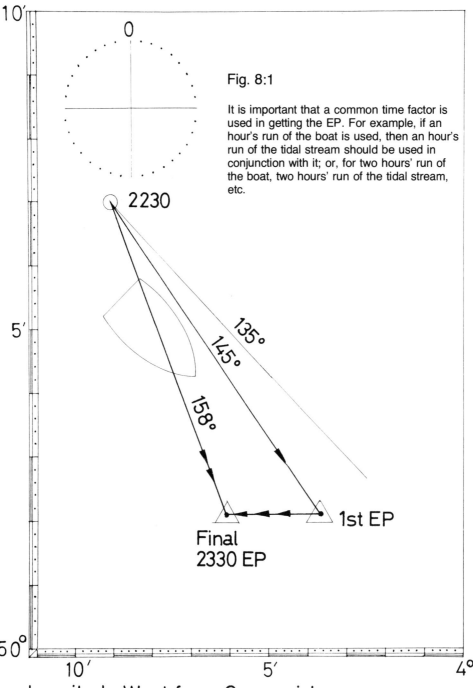

0

2230

Fig. 8:1

It is important that a common time factor is used in getting the EP. For example, if an hour's run of the boat is used, then an hour's run of the tidal stream should be used in conjunction with it; or, for two hours' run of the boat, two hours' run of the tidal stream, etc.

135°

145°

158°

1st EP

Final
2330 EP

10'

5'

50°

10'

5'

4°

Longitude West from Greenwich

Look at Fig. 8:1 which is a drawing of the plot done on the practice chart.

At 2230 a yacht is in an Observed Position 50°07'N   04°09'.1W. Her course is 135° and her estimated speed is about 6 knots. The wind is a steady NE force 4 and the leeway is reckoned to be about 10°. If the expected tidal stream for the next hour is 270° at 1.5 knots, what is the EP at 2330?

Now do what you learned in Unit 6 (Leeway). Plot the leeway track and measure 6 miles along it. That is the track the boat would have made had there been only the leeway and no tidal streams (145° for 6 miles). At this stage you will get the 1st EP 2330, which is 50°02'.1N   04°03'.7W.

NOW TO APPLY THE TIDAL STREAM.

From the 1st EP plot the tidal stream for 1 hour (270° at 1.5 knots). The final EP 2330 is at the end of the line marking the tidal stream, 50°02'.1N 04°06'.1W. Notice that the track made good is a line drawn between the 2230 fix and the final 2330 EP (two arrow heads). This track is about 158°.

Do the problem below (use the practice chart):

At 1230 a boat is in a position observed to be 50°01'.4N   04°09'.8W, heading on a course of 090°. Estimated speed is 4 knots and the wind is NE force 3. Leeway is about 10° and the estimated tidal stream is 270° at 2 knots. Which of the following positions is the 1330EP?

50°00'.7N   04°03'.7W . . . *page 111*
50°00'.7N   04°06'.8W . . . *page 109*

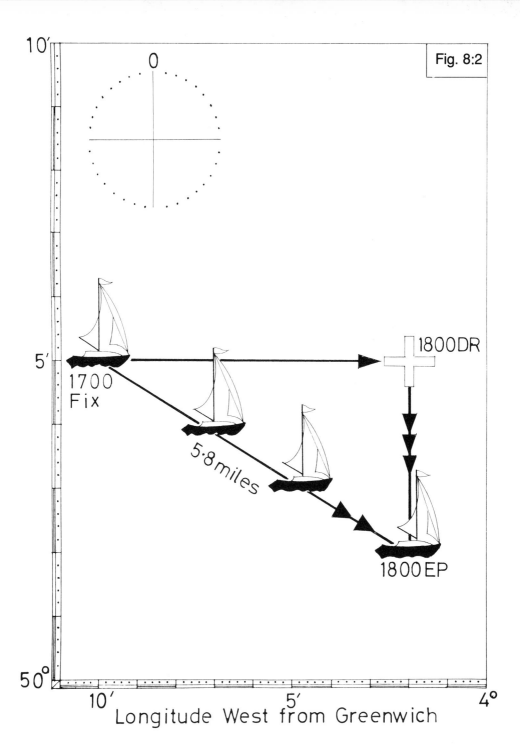

That last problem rounds off the method used in finding the EP when leeway and tidal streams are taken into consideration. There is one other situation which you are most likely to meet offshore and that is when there is no leeway to bother about (the wind is either dead ahead, astern or there is no wind at all). How do you plot the EP when only the tidal stream is expected?

The principle is very straightforward: plot the Observed Position, then the course line and the DR Position. From this point plot the tidal stream and the EP will be at the end of this line. That is, go straight to the final EP and miss out the 1st EP.

In Fig. 8:2 a yacht, running before the wind, is in an Observed Position 50°05′N   04°10′W at 1700. Her speed is 5 knots and course 090°, and the tidal stream expected between 1700 and 1800 is 180°, setting at a rate of 3 knots. What is the 1800 EP?

The Observed Position, course line (one arrow head) and DR Position 1800 are plotted. From the DR Position 1800 the tidal stream is plotted (three arrow heads). Remember to use the same time period for the distance run by the ship and the tidal stream drift. The EP at 1800 works out as 50°02′N 04°02′.2W.

Notice that the track made good is therefore 121° (this is marked by the succession of small yachts 'standing' on the line with two arrow heads). The actual distance made good, or the distance along the track made good, between 1700 and 1800 is 5.8 miles.

Try the following problem (use Fig. 8:2):

The skipper of motor yacht Spray *gets a reliable fix at 1945 which puts him in position 50°09′N   04°05′W. He calculates that, for the next hour at least, the mean tidal stream should be about 240° at 1 knot. He sets course 200° and expects to make a speed of about 2½ knots. What would be the 2045 EP (leeway is negligible)?*

EP 2045 is 50°06′.6N   04°06′.3W . . . *page 113*
EP 2045 is 50°06′.2N   04°07′.6W . . . *page 114*

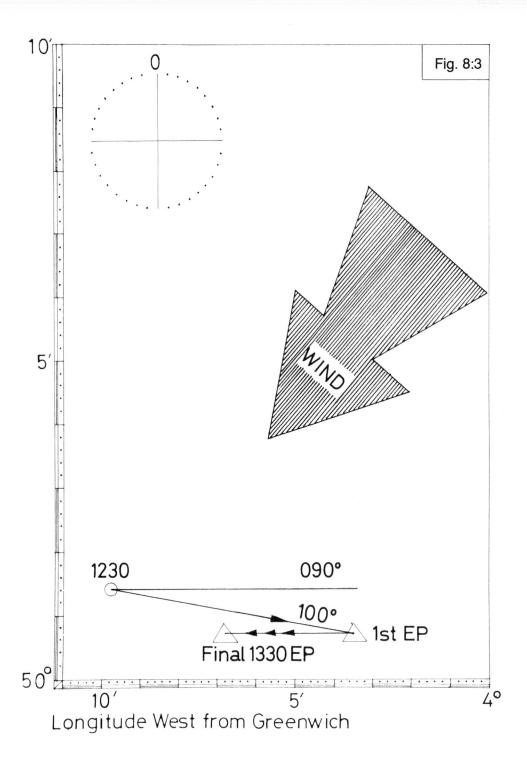

Fig. 8:3

Leeway track 330°. 1st EP 50°04'.6N 04°08'.3W Final EP 1515 50°03'.6N 04°10'.1W

In Fig. 8:3 is a run-down of the problem which you miscalculated
    There you can see the Observed Position at 1230, 50°01′.4N   04°09′.8W, the leeway track, which is 100° (the wind is coming from the NE), the 1st EP, and the Final 1330 EP which is 50°00′.7N   04°06′.8W.
    Just for good measure do the following problem:
        At 1415 a boat is sailing on a course of 340° and the skipper gets a fix 50°02′N   04°06′W. During the past hour the distance measured by log was 3 miles. The wind is NE force 3 and the estimated leeway 10°. The expected tidal stream during the period 1415 to 1615 is 230° at 1.5 knots. If the ocurse and speed is maintained what position could the skipper reasonably expect to be in at 1515?

Work this problem out first and then refer to the answers at the bottom of the opposite page. After you have done that return to page 107.

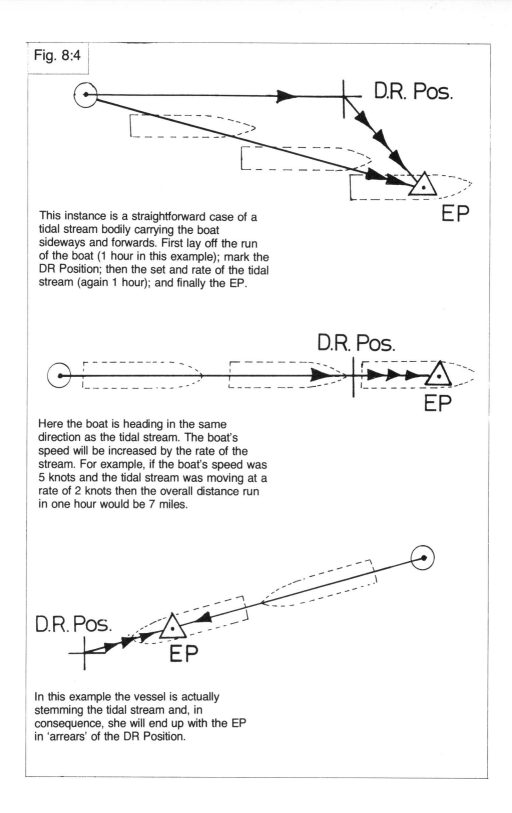

Fig. 8:4

D.R. Pos.

EP

This instance is a straightforward case of a tidal stream bodily carrying the boat sideways and forwards. First lay off the run of the boat (1 hour in this example); mark the DR Position; then the set and rate of the tidal stream (again 1 hour); and finally the EP.

D.R. Pos.

EP

Here the boat is heading in the same direction as the tidal stream. The boat's speed will be increased by the rate of the stream. For example, if the boat's speed was 5 knots and the tidal stream was moving at a rate of 2 knots then the overall distance run in one hour would be 7 miles.

D.R. Pos.

EP

In this example the vessel is actually stemming the tidal stream and, in consequence, she will end up with the EP in 'arrears' of the DR Position.

NOTE: THE SAME PERIOD OF TIME FOR THE DISTANCE RUN BY THE BOAT AND THE TIDAL STREAM DRIFT MUST BE OBSERVED.

You got the DR Position and the EP confused.

Have a good look at the three examples on the opposite page (Fig. 8:4). In all cases the procedure is the same.

1. Plot the Observed Position.
2. Plot the boat's course line.
3. Plot the DR Position.
4. Mark off the tidal stream set and rate FROM the DR Position.
5. The EP required is at the end of the tidal stream line.

Move on to page 114 when you are sure that you understand these examples. If you are unsure of the principles return to page 109 and re-think the problem.

☑ *You are doing well if you came straight here from page 109*

Summary

a) Plot the Observed Position as a 'starter'
b) Next plot the course line and along it the DR Position (as though there was no wind or tidal stream to carry you off that line).
c) If there is leeway influencing your progress plot the leeway track and then an EP along it (call this the 1st EP).
d) Apply the tidal stream to the 1st EP to get the final EP.
e) If there is no tidal stream influence then the 1st EP is the one you want.
f) If there is no wind and thus no leeway then go straight to the final EP. The overall track made good is from the fix to the final EP.
g) The tidal stream is marked with three arrow heads.
h) REMEMBER THAT THE ESTIMATED POSITION IS A FUTURE POSITION AND IS, AT BEST, APPROXIMATE.

Try your hand at doing Exercise 8 on the next page

Exercise 8

To do this exercise you will need to refer to the Tide Tables on page 94. All times quoted here are B.S.T. unless otherwise stated. Some of the questions involve plotting the Observed Position, the EP with both leeway and tidal streams taken into consideration, and the EP with just the tidal stream taken into account. The following questions are all part of a continuing problem and they involve a small boat sailing just off Looe.

9 July 1975. A ketch is sailing about 2 miles to the SSW of St George's Island (Looe). The wind is NE force 4 and the visibility is excellent.

a) At 0633 bearings are taken as follows:
    Coast Guard Flag Staff (CGFS) Polperro 306°
    RHE St George's Island 034°
    What is the 0633 Obs. Pos?
b) At 0633 course is set for the Eddystone Light House. The estimated speed of the yacht is 4 knots. Leeway is about 12°. The log reads 11.9. What is the 0733 EP?
c) At 0730 the yacht's position by observation is 50°15'.9N   04°23'.1W. The log reads 16, and the wind veers to the E, force 3. The skipper decides to alter course to 290°. The spinnaker is hoisted and the boat's speed increases to an estimated 6 knots. There is no leeway.
    What is the 0830 EP?
d) At 0830 the following bearings are taken:
    RHE St George's Island 046°
    Coast Guard Flag Staff (CGFS) Polperro 349°
    Beacon (near Shag Rock) 308°
    Speed is still estimated at 6 knots. The log reads 22.1 and the course is altered to 260°.
    1.   What is the 0830 Obs. Pos.?
    2.   What is the 0930 EP?
e) Do you think that bearings of the beacon (west of Lantic Bay) and the church tower (ruins; Polruan) provide a reliable 'fix'?

Answers overleaf

Answers: Exercise 8

a) 0633 fix 50°18'.7N   04°28'.2W.

b) Plot the course, which is 135°. Plot the leeway track (147°). The 1st EP (just taking leeway into account) is 50°15'.3N   04°24'.8W. Then plot the tidal stream from the 1st EP. HW time 9 July 1975 is 0538 G.M.T. (0638 B.S.T.) (Springs). The predominant tidal streams throughout the 0633-0733 period relate to ⟨F⟩ . The tidal stream between 0633 and 0733 is the mean between HW and 1 hour after HW. HW is 072° at 0.9 knots and 1 hour after HW is 084° at 0.9 knots. Therefore mean tidal stream is 078° at 0.9 knots. Final EP is 50°15'.5N   04°23'.4W.

c) Plot the course line and the 0830 DR Pos. which is 50°18'N   04°31'.9W. Now find out the mean tidal stream running between 0730 and 0830. At 0730 the time is 1 hour after HW and the stream is 084° at 0.9 knots. At 0830 the stream is 103° at 0.6 knots. The mean tidal stream is therefore about 094° at 0.8 knots. This stream, plotted from the DR Pos., gives the 0830 EP which is 50°17'.9N   04°30'.7W.

d) 1. Obs. Pos. 0830 50°18'N   04°30'.2W.
    2. 0930 DR Pos. 50°16'.9N   04°39'.4W. The tidal streams still refer to ⟨F⟩ .

    From this position plot the mean tidal stream influence. At 0830 (2 hours after HW) the stream is 103° at 0.6 knots. At 0930 (3 hours after HW) the stream is 136° at 0.4 knots. The tidal stream between 0830 and 0930 is the mean of these, which is 120° at about 0.5 knots. The 0930 EP is therefore 50°16'.6N   04°38'.7W.

e) The angle of 'cut' would be something like 20° and this is far too narrow to provide reliability. You'd be better off using marks such as Gribbin Head and Pencarrow Head.

This unit wasn't easy and you have probably crossed one of the worst hurdles. Please carry on to the next unit.

UNIT 9 Magnetism: Variation

In previous units we have learned how to

     measure distances
     measure speeds
     read a chart
     define courses and tracks
     get a position line and take a fix
     plot the DR Position
     find tidal streams information and apply it
     find leeway and apply it
     plot the EP

but we have not yet learnt how to take into account Variation and Deviation in our calculations. This has been done deliberately to avoid confusing you, because this often happens if these subjects are introduced too soon. In practical terms, as far as the navigator is concerned all Variation and Deviation amount to is the need for the addition or subtraction of a small figure to or from a course or bearing.

Variation and Deviation are considered separately in this programme. Variation is the subject of this unit and Deviation will be dealt with in Unit 11.

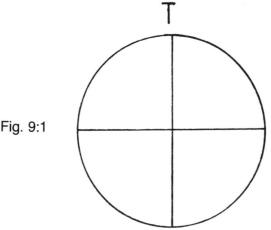

Fig. 9:1

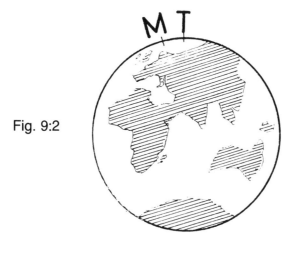

Fig. 9:2

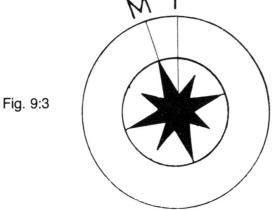

Fig. 9:3

Up to now in the programme 'North' has been used as a reference which we have used in doing our chartwork. This 'North' could more accurately be called 'TRUE NORTH'. It is also referred to as 'Geographic North'. Fig. 9:1 shows True North marked as 'T'.

There is another North to be taken into account, MAGNETIC NORTH. It is because of the nature of the earth's magnetic field that Magnetic North is not the same as True North. In Fig. 9:2 Magnetic North is labelled 'M'.

If a compass card with a magnet attached to it is pivoted on a point so that it may swing freely the magnet will 'hunt' for and finally settle so that it points in the direction of Magnetic North (Fig. 9:3). A ship's compass is of course more complicated than this, but the basic principle is the same.

Page 121 now

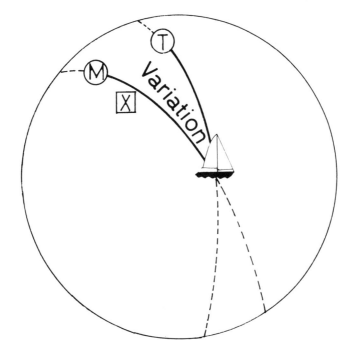

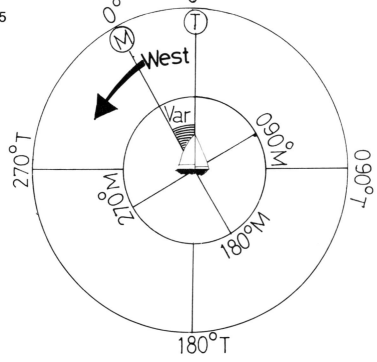

The angle between the direction of Magnetic North and True North is called the VARIATION (Fig. 9:4)

The amount of Variation changes from one part of the earth to another. A change in the heading of a ship does not affect the variation, only a move from one sailing area to another.

Fig. 9:5 is another way of representing what is shown in Fig. 9:4. The two lines of direction are still from the sloop but now we can focus our attention on whether the Variation is west or east. Well, it is clearly west in this case because the Magnetic North would be to the west of True North.

Now return to Fig. 9:4. Is the variation at the position of 'X' less than the variation at the yacht? Would it be 'variation east' or 'variation west'?

All secrets are unfolded on page 123

Fig. 9:6

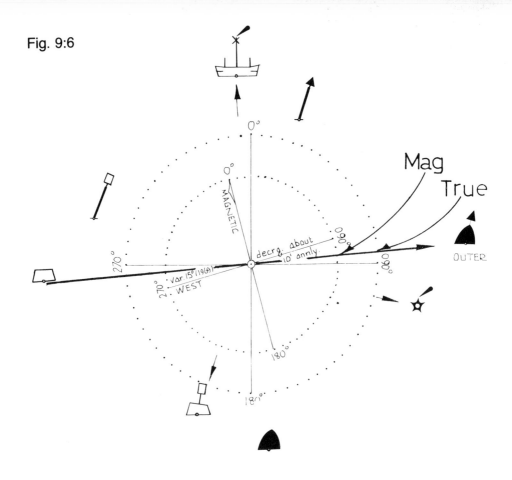

	Departure	Destination	True Course	Variation	Magnetic Course
a			085°T	15°W	100°M
b				15°W	
c				15°W	
d				15°W	

The Variation at 'X' is more than the Variation at the yacht. In both cases it is 'Variation west'.

The Magnetic North Pole is not a constant location. It moves gradually and over many years shifts its position. We can state that in any particular area of the earth the Variation will vary from year to year.

Fig. 9:6 shows a compass rose and on it, as on the majority of compass roses, you can see four items that are of interest at this stage:
1. The outer (TRUE) rose.
2. The inner (MAGNETIC) rose.
3. Information as to the amount and direction of the Variation (here 15°W).
4. The year when that Variation applies and the annual rate of change (here 1969 decreasing about 10′ annually).

Now assume that, in 1969, a boat is sailing somewhere in the vicinity of this compass rose and, starting off from the port hand (can) buoy, it sets course in the direction of the starboard hand buoy (with topmark). There is no wind or tidal stream. What would be the Magnetic course to steer? Before you attempt an answer read on.

We can plot the True course (this diagram is designed so that you can lay a straight edge from one mark to the other and this will pass right through the centre of the compass rose, without your having to bother about using parallel rulers). The True course is then recorded as 085°T.

Since we are operating in the same year as that printed on the compass rose (1969) the Magnetic course may be read straight off the inner Magnetic, rose. The Magnetic course is 100°M.

Complete the table opposite putting in the True and the Magnetic courses. The year of operation is 1969 throughout the exercise. After this is completed carry on reading.

Fig. 9:7

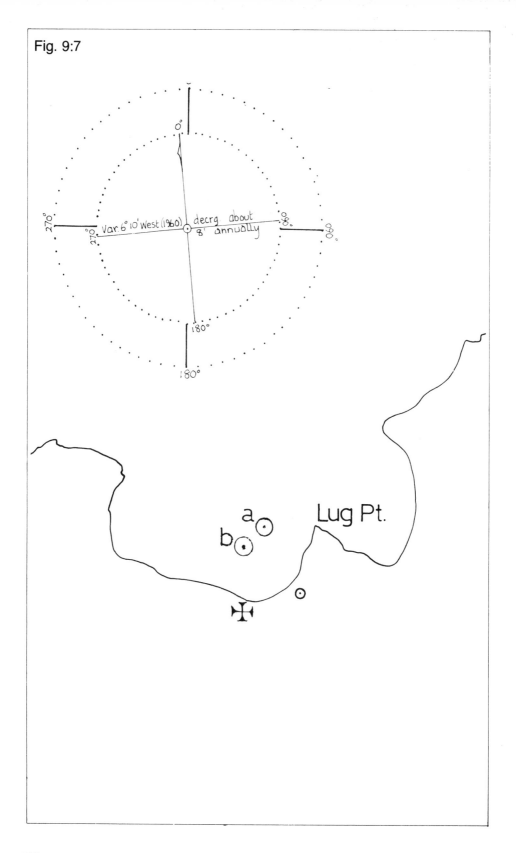

Var. 6° 10' West (1960) decrg about 8' annually

270°

0°

90°

180°

a

b

Lug Pt.

You should have got the following:

	True course	Variation	Magnetic course
a)	085°T	15°W	100°M
b)	355°T	15°W	010°M
c)	200°T	15°W	215°M
d)	105°T	15°W	120°M

By observation of the results we can see that when we want to convert a True course to a Magnetic course, we add if the variation is westerly. We could in fact have put a plus sign in front of the Variation (i.e. '+ 15°W'). If the Variation had been east instead of west then we would have subtracted it when going from TRUE to MAGNETIC. Consider the next problem.

> A boat is heading on a course of 200°T. The Variation is 10° east. What is the Magnetic course?

If the principle of + west and − east is applied when changing True courses into Magnetic courses, then we must substract 10° easterly Variation from the True course and this gives a Magnetic course of 190°M (200°T −10°E = 190°M).

Every example we have discussed up till now has dealt exclusively with the problem of converting courses from True to Magnetic, and that is as it should be. After all, the first line drawn on the chart is the required track and this is always True. But there are instances when a skipper must convert a Magnetic course to a True course in order that he may plot on the chart where his boat has been. For example:

> At 1753 a skipper fixes his position, turns to a crew member and instructs him to steer 155°M. He then goes below to listen to the weather forecast and leaves the helmsman to his job. After about 20 minutes the skipper, as a double check, asks the other what course he has been steering and this turns out to be 145°M due to a misunderstanding between the two concerned. So the skipper turns to and plots the corrected course line on the chart. Assuming that there has been no wind or tidal influences throughout and the Variation is 7°W, what was the True Course steered?

We have already learned that when going from True to Magnetic we must +west and −east variations. But in this example we have to convert from Magnetic to True so we REVERSE THE PROCEDURE (−west and +east). The course steered is 145°M and if the variation of 7° west is taken away from the Magnetic course then the True course steered must be 138°T.

The same applies when converting Magnetic bearings to True bearings. Try the next problem (use Fig. 9:7)

At 1350 on 12 August 1975 the owner of a small craft sailing in the area SW of Lug Point uses the handbearing compass to get the following bearings:
LHE Lug Point 079°M   Chimney 129°M   Church 184°M
What is the 1350 fix?

1350 fix is at position 'a' . . . *page 127*
1350 fix is at position 'b' . . . *page 128*

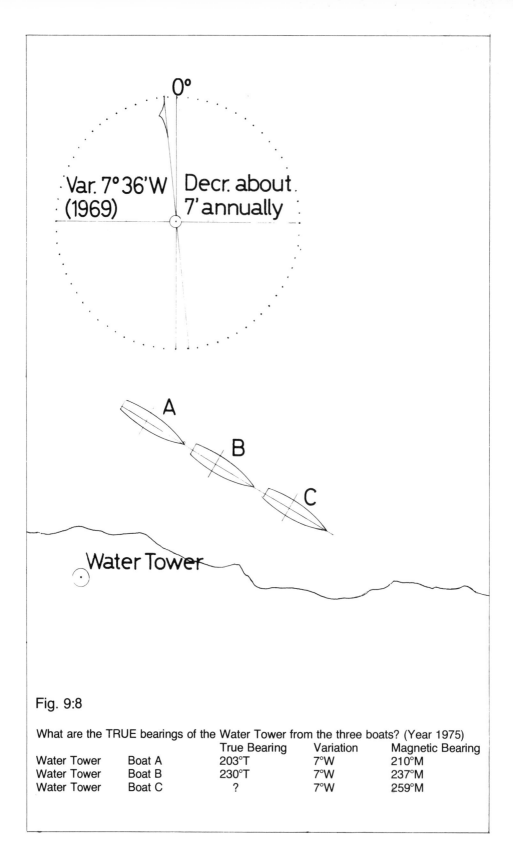

Fig. 9:8

What are the TRUE bearings of the Water Tower from the three boats? (Year 1975)

		True Bearing	Variation	Magnetic Bearing
Water Tower	Boat A	203°T	7°W	210°M
Water Tower	Boat B	230°T	7°W	237°M
Water Tower	Boat C	?	7°W	259°M

(Did you remember to take into account the decrease in the Variation between 1960 and 1975?)

However, don't concern yourself too much because where insight into principles evades us there is usually a way of overcoming the difficulty. But before we do any more let's just put things into perspective. Because the Variation around the British Isles happens to be westerly then all we have to do is plot the True course and then ADD ON ANY VARIATION WHICH EXISTS (5°, 6° or something of that order). So all in all Variation interferes with our pleasure only to the extent of our having to add a small figure to a another. If we are taking bearings then we subtract a small figure from another.

Remember the word MADET. It is an aid to memory and indicates how to apply the Variation. It means Magnetic ADd East True or , more fully, MAGNETIC TO TRUE ADD EAST. This is a starting point from which you can work out the other 'rules': MAGNETIC TO TRUE ADD EAST (AND SUBTRACT WEST).

Just to reinforce the idea look at the following diagram:

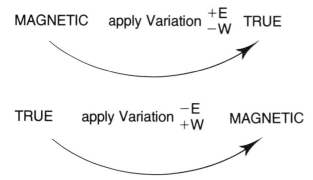

MAGNETIC   apply Variation $^{+E}_{-W}$ TRUE

TRUE   apply Variation $^{-E}_{+W}$ MAGNETIC

Now follow the example on the opposite page and then carry on to page 128

Summary

a) Variation is the angle between TRUE North and MAGNETIC North.
b) Variation is registered as west or east.
c) The Variation depends upon your location.
d) Sometimes you can plot straight off the Magnetic rose on a chart if the 'Variation date' is close to the year of operation.
e) A change of heading on the part of the boat does not alter the Variation.
f) When going from True to Magnetic, +west and −east.
g) When going from Magnetic to True, −west and +east.

Do Exercise 9 on the next page. However, if you would like to do more work on this subject before going on to do the exercise then you may find that page 126 may be of interest (that is, if you haven't already done that page).

'Now we've sorted out the Variation our problems are over.'

Exercise 9

The following questions are part of a continuing problem which deals with auxiliary yacht *Stealaway* on passage from Falmouth to Fowey. Tidal streams are always given as a True direction and the Variation you should use is found on the compass rose nearest the scene of operations. You will need to refer to the Tide Tables on page 94. As usual all times quoted here are B.S.T.

a) At 1430 on 8 August 1975, course steered is 078°M. The wind is NW force 3 and the log reads 4.3. At 1530 the log reads 8.9 and bearings are taken as follows:
LHE Nare Head 281°M   RHE Dodman Point 054°M
Caerhays Catle 003°M
What is the 1530 fix?

b) At 1530 an alteration of course is made to 085°M. The wind is N force 4 and the speed is estimated to have increased to about 5.5 knots. The leeway is about 10°. What will be the 1600 EP?

c) At 1550 the skipper decides to re-check his position and gets Nare Head 284°M and RHE Dodman Point 005°M. The log reads 10.7. What is the 1550 fix?

d) The course is altered to 044°M and the speed is now 5 knots. The leeway is 15°. Assuming the tidal streams to be at slack water what will be the 1650 EP?

e) At 1650 another fix is taken as follows:
        LHE Dodman Point 255°M
        Mevagissey Light 294°M
        LHE Black Head 326°M
What is the 1650 fix?

f) If the difference between the 1650 EP and 1650 fix is due to tidal influences what would have been the direction and rate of the streams during the period 1550-1650?

g) From the 1650 Obs. Pos. what will be the ground track required to reach the bell buoy off Fowey Harbour?

Answers on the next page

Answers: Exercise 9

The chart gives 1974 Variation, which is appropriate for 1975, so you can read straight off the Magnetic rose if you wish. To be exact Variation in 1975 would be taken from the compass rose situated just to the SE of Falmouth. The 1974 figure is 8°40'W (decreasing about 5' annually). The precise Variation for 1975 would therefore be 8°35'W (9° will do).

a) 1530 fix is 50°11'.6N 04°50'.3W.
b) Variation 9°W applied to a course of 085°M gives us 076°T. The leeway track is 086°T. HW is at 1836 G.M.T. (1936 B.S.T.). The tides are at Springs. Tidal streams at ◇E 1530 (4 hours before HW) are slack. At 1630 (3 hours before HW) they are 077° at 0.2 knots. For all intents and purposes slack will do. 1600 EP is therefore 50°11'.8N 04°45'.9W.
c) To convert LHE Nare Head 284°M subtract Variation 9°W to get 275°T. To convert RHE Dodman Point 005°M subtract Variation 9°W to get 356°T. 1550 fix is 50°11'.3N   04°47'.6W.
d) Converting 044°M by subtracting Variation 9°W we get 035°T. Plot the leeway track 050°T. 1650 EP is 50°14'.5N   04°41'.6W.
e) Convert LHE Dodman Point 255°M by subtracting Variation 9°W to get 246°T. Mevagissey Light 294°M becomes 285°T and LHE Black Head 317°T. 1650 fix is 50°15'.1N   04°41'.1W.
f) The tidal stream 1550-1650 is 027° at 0.6 knots.
g) Required ground track 014°T.

If you managed to get most of the correct answers, well done. But most important is that you understand the reason why if you got individual answers wrong.

UNIT 10
Counteracting Tidal Streams & Wind

It's all very well being pushed around by tidal and wind influences but there are many occasions when you have to take pains to counter their effect. The tidal stream will be the first factor to come under scrutiny.

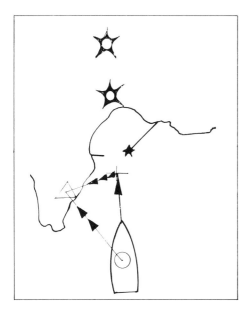

Fig. 10:1

Here the boat's skipper has tried to make the harbour but the boat has been swept to the SW by tidal streams. He has done everything you have been taught to do – plotted the fix, course, DR Position, tidal stream and EP – and unfortunately he's gone and run his craft aground.

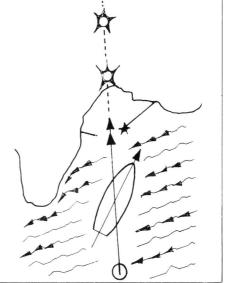

Fig. 10:2

But in this case the skipper has kept the two leading lights in line (they are there to 'see' a boat into the harbour). But in order to do so he has had to alter course. Notice in both illustrations the different courses.

The main concern in this unit is to calculate accurately which course is the right one to steer in order to make good the required track. In other words what happens when there are no leading marks conveniently placed to help the navigator along?

Page 133

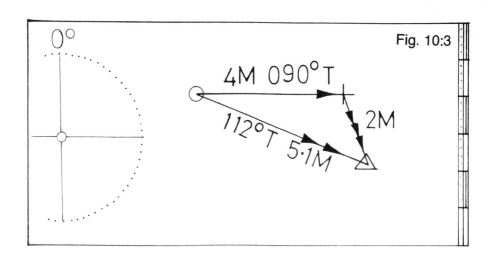

Fig. 10:3

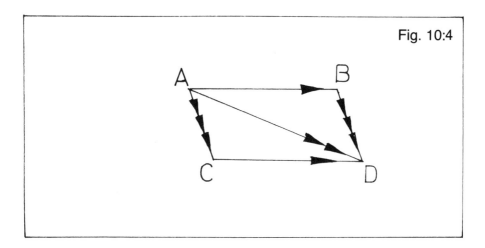

Fig. 10:4

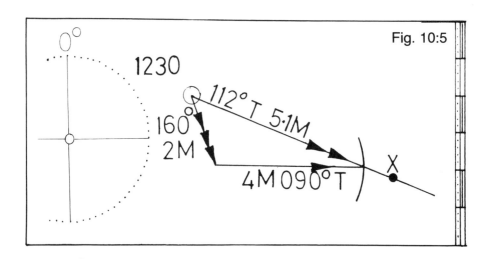

Fig. 10:5

Now please turn back to page 90 (Fig. 7:1) and recall the message which that illustration gave. This was plotting the course line from the fix, then marking the DR Position, next drawing in the tidal stream and finally the Estimated Position. In particular notice the TRACK MADE GOOD which is marked very plainly in the diagram.

In Fig. 10:3 a similar diagram (a triangle) is shown. This is called a 'triangle of velocities'. If you are given two sides of this triangle then the other side is the result of the previous two. The known sides are the course line (in this case 1 hour's run for 4 miles at 090°T) and the tidal stream (1 hour's run for 2 miles at 160°). The Track Made Good is the result of the boat's course and speed and the tidal stream direction and rate.

Fig. 10:4 gives the same triangle and adds two more lines. We now have a parallelogram in which the Track Made Good (AD) is seen to be the resultant of AC and CD, which are the same in length and direction as the original course line and tidal stream line. In this unit the bottom triangle ACD is the thing we shall concentrate on. But let's get back to sea (on the bottom triangle if you will!). Look at Fig. 10:5, where at 1230 a small launch is in an Observed Position and the skipper REQUIRES TO MAKE GOOD TRACK 112°T. The destination is position 'X'. Her speed is 4 knots and the expected tidal stream for 2 hours is 160° at 2 knots.

How does he find the Course To Steer to make good the Required Track?
1. From the Observed Position plot the required track and the tidal stream direction and rate. The stream runs 2 miles in 1 hour (i.e. 2 knots).
2. Now use the third factor, which is the boat's speed, and drawn in 1 hour's run of the vessel FROM THE END OF THE TIDAL STREAM. This is done by using the distance run as the radius of an arc which cuts the required track. The line joining the end of the tidal stream to this 'cut' is the COURSE TO STEER to make good the required track (thus Course To Steer is 090°).

To complete the picture we can say that the distance made good over the ground in 1 hour is 5.1 miles. Since the distance from the 1230 position to 'X' is 6 miles then the Estimated Time of Arrival (ETA) at 'X' is 1340 (1230 + 6 ÷ 5.1 hours = 1230 + 1 hour 10 minutes).

Now use chart 5050 to do the next problem.

At 1330 a small fishing boat is in Obs. Pos. 50°10'N 04°41'W and the navigator requires to make good a track of 085°T. The estimated speed of the vessel is 6 knots and the expected tidal stream during the next hour is 100° at 2 knots. What course would he order to be set to make sure that the track tequired is made good? How far would she travel over the ground in 1 hour? What would be the ETA at position 50°11'.2N 04°20'W?

080°T   7.9 miles ETA 1512 . . . *page 137*
077°T   6.0 miles ETA 1545 . . . *page 135*

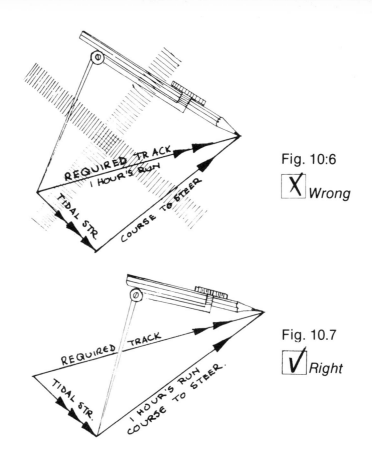

Fig. 10:6

X Wrong

Fig. 10.7

✓ Right

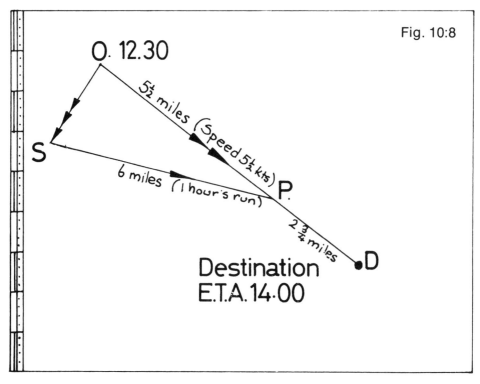

Fig. 10:8

O. 12.30

5½ miles (Speed 5½ kts)

S

6 miles (1 hour's run)

P.

2¾ miles

D

Destination
E.T.A. 14·00

Course 077°T is wrong because the hour's run of 6 miles was measured from the starting position (Obs. Pos.) and not from the end of the tidal stream. The correct course to steer was 080°T, and distance travelled in 1 hour was 7.9 miles. You should go back and check this statement.

In Figs. 10:6 and 10:7 both wrong and right methods are shown.

Refer to Fig. 10:8 and see what you make of the next problem.

A boat in position 'O' requires to make good a track OD. Her speed is 6 knots and you can see that the course she must steer to make good the track OD is SP. The tidal stream is of course OS.

The actual distance covered in 1 hour – the mark scratched on the sea bed if the boat's keel was just touching it – is $5\frac{1}{2}$ miles (OP). Thus the vessel's effective speed *over the ground* is $5\frac{1}{2}$ knots.

Now, in all, the distance between the boat's departure position and her destination is $8\frac{1}{4}$ miles (OD = $8\frac{1}{4}$). Since it takes 1 hour to travel $5\frac{1}{2}$ miles then it will take $1\frac{1}{2}$ hours to get to the destination if the tidal stream continues to run at the same rate and in the same direction. Half an hour's run is $2\frac{3}{4}$ miles ($5\frac{1}{2}$ miles + $2\frac{3}{4}$ miles = $8\frac{1}{4}$).

The Estimated Time of Arrival (ETA) is therefore 1230 hours + $1\frac{1}{2}$ hours = 1400 hours.

Page 137 next

Fig. 10:9

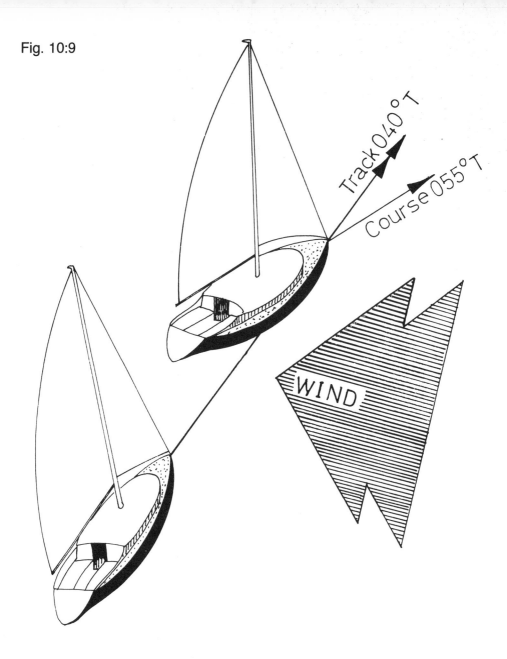

Track 040°T

Course 055°T

WIND

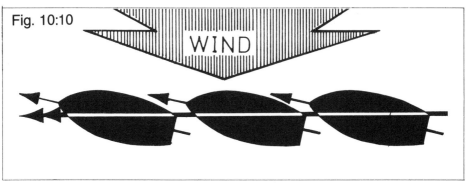

Fig. 10:10

WIND

Good work. Having allowed for the tidal stream, we can now sort out the leeway. But before this is done it will be helpful to re-cap on the passage planning thus far.

1. The required track has been drawn.
2. The tidal stream has been allowed for; the boat's head has been altered so that the stream has been counteracted.
3. The stage reached here is that we have a TRUE COURSE and it is to this TRUE COURSE that the leeway is applied.

When dealing with the leeway the ship's head has to be altered so that the required track is made good.

In Fig. 10:9 a boat's skipper wants to make good a required track of 040°T. The wind is easterly and sufficiently strong to cause the craft to make 15° of leeway. There is slack water and thus no tidal stream.

The vessel has to 'luff' into the wind in order to stay on her track. The course she should steer in order to do this will have to be 055°T (the wind is hitting her on the starboard side – she is said to be on the starboard tack).

In Fig. 10:10 may be seen the way in which a boat would have to 'crab' sideways along her track if she wished to keep on it in spite of the leeway.

A small yacht wishes to make good a track of 180°T. She is on the port tack (wind on the port side) and is making 10° leeway. She has already allowed for a tidal stream. Which of the following courses should she steer to maintain the track of 180°T?

170°T . . . *page 139*
190°T . . . *page 141*

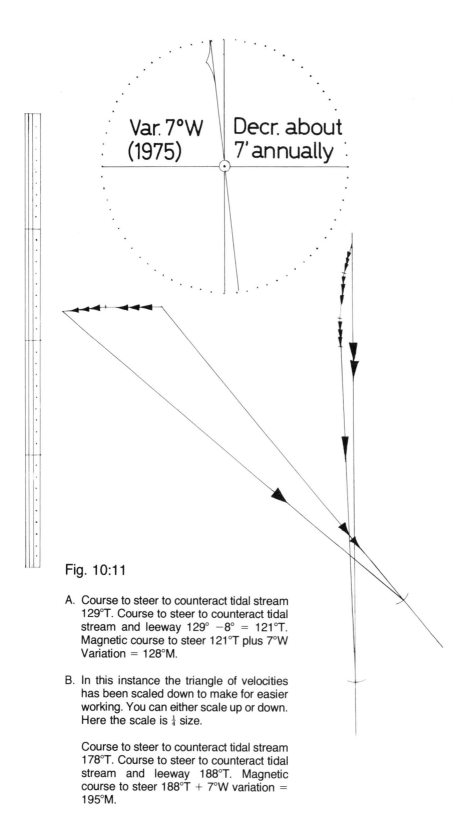

Fig. 10:11

A. Course to steer to counteract tidal stream 129°T. Course to steer to counteract tidal stream and leeway 129° −8° = 121°T. Magnetic course to steer 121°T plus 7°W Variation = 128°M.

B. In this instance the triangle of velocities has been scaled down to make for easier working. You can either scale up or down. Here the scale is ¼ size.

Course to steer to counteract tidal stream 178°T. Course to steer to counteract tidal stream and leeway 188°T. Magnetic course to steer 188°T + 7°W variation = 195°M.

In the compass rose:

Var. 7°W (1975)

Decr. about 7' annually

We have been using 1 hour's run of vessel in conjunction with 1 hour's tidal stream influences; this was for simplicity. It is however normal to plan a passage for several hours. For example:

A boat leaves a position at 1545 and the skipper wishes to make good a track of 280°T. The speed is 2 knots. There is no leeway, and tidal streams are as follows: 1545–1645 180° at 0.8 knots, 1645–1745 230° at 1.0 knot, 1745–1845 250° at 1.2 knots.

What would be the course to steer from 1545 to 1845 to make good track 280°T?

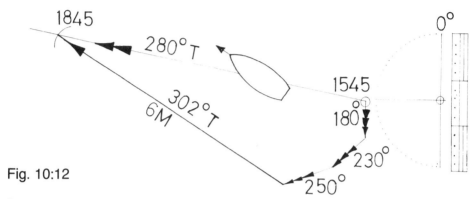

Fig. 10:12

Plot the three successive streams from the 1545 position. Then treat them as though they were just one total stream; that is, from the end of the last stream scribe a distance of 3 HOURS's RUN OF CRAFT and where this intersects the track make a mark. Join up the end of the stream vector to the mark made on the track. This will be the course required to make good track 280°T.

It is important to remember that the time period for the distance run by the vessel must be the same as the time period for the tidal stream drift; so if, as in the instance above, 3 hours' tidal steam is used then you must also use 3 hours' run of craft. It is also necessary that you maintain a consistent speed – any change of wind will upset the arrangement.

Try to do the following examples. The answers and plots are opposite. You should try to do the examples before consulting page 138.

A. 14 July 1975. At 1345 a skipper requires to make good a track of 140°T. The boat's speed is a steady 2 knots. Tidal streams expected are as follows: 1345–1445 270° at 0.5 knots. 1445–1545 265° at 0.4 knots. The wind is NE 4. Leeway is about 8°. What is the Magnetic course to steer for the next two hours in order to make good track 140°T?

B. 25 September 1975. At 1930 it is decided that a track of 180°T is required in order to clear hazards ahead. Wind is W force 3. Leeway is estimated at 10°. The boat's speed is estimated as 4 knots. The tidal streams expected during the next three hours are 195° at 1.0 knots, 185° at 1.6 knots, 180° at 1.0 knots. What would be the Magnetic course to steer to make good track 180°T from 1930 to 2230?

Move to page 142

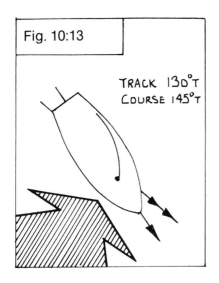

Fig. 10:13

TRACK 130°T
COURSE 145°T

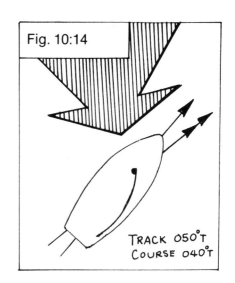

Fig. 10:14

TRACK 050°T
COURSE 040°T

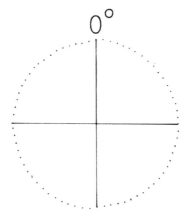

0°

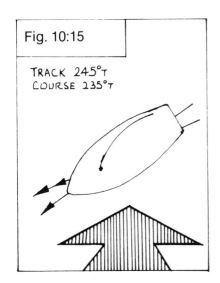

Fig. 10:15

TRACK 245°T
COURSE 235°T

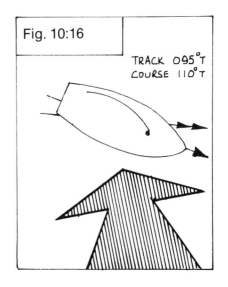

Fig. 10:16

TRACK 095°T
COURSE 110°T

$\boxed{\text{X}}$ *190° T is wrong*

If you are ever in doubt about which way to apply the leeway, start with the realisation of exactly which side of the boat the wind is hitting.

In Fig. 10:13 the wind is hitting the starboard side of the boat (she is on the starboard tack and her sails are out to port). In this instance the leeway is added to the required track because the boat has to alter course to starboard if the track of 130° is to be maintained.

In Fig. 10:14 the vessel is on the port tack and the leeway is subtracted from the required track.

You will notice that when a boat is on the port tack leeway is subtracted (Fig. 10:15) and when a craft is on the starboard tack leeway is added to the required track (Fig. 10:16).

Page 137

Summary

a) In some situations it may be necessary to alter the ship's head in order to counteract tidal streams or leeway or both.

b) It is possible to work out the course to steer to counteract a tidal stream which spans a period of several hours, always providing that you use a time period of distance run which is the same as that for the tidal drift.

c) When both tidal stream and leeway are counteracted at the same time, the stream is sorted out first and a True course obtained. Then the leeway is applied to this course and finally any Variation is taken into account.

Exercise 10 below includes problems which deal with all the principles discussed in this unit.

Exercise 10

As usual, this exercise represents a continuing problem. Remember tidal stream directions are always True – use the compass rose near the scene of operations to find the appropriate Variation.

a) 8 August 1975. At 1010 auxiliary yacht *Barnacle* is on passage from Newton Ferrers to Looe. The wind is NNE force 3. The visibility is about 10 miles and the log reads 6.3. The following bearings are taken:

    LHE Rame Head 298°M
    Plymouth Breakwater (Beacon, Eastern edge) 051°M
    RHE Penlee Point 355°M

What is the 1010 fix?   *50 18 1 N 04 10 9 W*

b) At 1010 a course of 286°M is set, and the leeway is estimated at about 8°. The estimated speed is 3 knots. What is the 1110 EP? (You should consider leeway to get the first EP and the tidal streams to get the final EP).

c) The next reliable fix was taken at 1120 when the following bearings were recorded:

    RHE Rame Head 092°M
    Portwrinkle Tower 005°M
    Beacon (50°21'.1N   04°16'.1W) 034°M

What was the 1120 fix?

d) At 1120 the wind is still NNE force 3, but it is freshening slightly. The log is 10.4. An alteration of course to 303°M is made, and the speed is increased to 3½ knots. The leeway is now 10°. What is the 1220 EP?

e) At 1230 the boat's Observed Position was found to be 50°19'.1N 04°24'.6W. The skipper decides to alter course for Fowey. What course would he have to steer to make good a track for the bell buoy SW of Fowey? The leeway is now 8° and the log is 14. The estimated speed is again 3 knots. Assuming the speed remains steady then it should take about three hours to reach the buoy. You should consider 'counteracting the tides' for three hours.

f) What is the Estimated Time of Arrival (ETA) at the buoy?

Answers on following pages

Answers: Exercise 10

a) LHE Rame Head 298°M Variation 8°W 290°T
  Plymouth Breakwater Beacon (Eastern edge) 051°M Variation 8°W 043°T.
  RHE Penlee Point 355°M Variation 8°W 347°T.
  1010 fix 50°18′.1N   04°10′.9W.
(In this item the Magnetic bearings have been converted to True by calculation. There is no need to do this because the year in question, 1975, is close enough to the year when the chart was printed. The Magnetic rose may be used directly but beware of charts which are significantly out of date.)

b) The leeway track is 270°T. The 1110 1st EP is 50°18′.1N   04°15′.6W.
  HW Devonport on 8 August 1975 is 0617 G.M.T. (0717 B.S.T.). The tides are at Springs. The tidal diamond referred to is Ⓖ.
    1010 (3 hours after HW) 235° at 0.3 knots
    1110 (4 hours after HW) 242° at 0.8 knots
    1010–1110 mean tidal stream is 238° at 0.6 knots
    1110 final EP 50°17′.8N   04°16′.4W

c) 1120 fix 50°18′.3N   04°18′.2W.

d) Leeway track 285°T. 1220 1st EP 50°19′.2N   04°23′.4W.
  To sort out the tidal streams you need to know
  1. What the streams are doing at 1120 (4 hours after HW) at the position of the boat (which is about midway between Ⓕ and Ⓖ .)
    4 hours after at Ⓕ   207° at 0.3 knots
    4 hours after Ⓖ   242° at 0.8 knots
    Tidal stream 1120 is 225° at 0.6 knots.
  2. As the yacht sails more to the west she comes more and more under the influence of the stream at Ⓕ   so what you now want is information about streams at Ⓕ   at 1220 (5 hours after HW). These are 241° at 0.6 knots. To find the stream from the 1120 fix and the 1220 EP we work as follows:
    1120 225° at 0.6 knots
    1220 241° at 0.6 knots
    1120–1220 stream is 233° at 0.6 knots
  Final 1120 EP 50°18′.8N   04°24′.2W.

e) The required track is 265°T. Since, at 1230, the craft is about 9½ miles (3 hours' run) away from the buoy off Fowey we should work out the tidal stream for the period 1230–1530. All information is referred to Ⓕ which is the closest diamond.
    1230 (5 hours after HW) 241° at 0.6 knots
    1330 (6 hours after HW) 249° at 0.8 knots
  1230–1330 mean tidal stream is 245° at 0.7 knots
  We are between HW's now so change to next HW, which is 1836 G.M.T. (1936 B.S.T.)
    1330 (6 hours before HW) 253° at 0.8 knots
    1430 (5 hours before HW) 270° at 0.7 knots
    1330–1430 mean tidal stream is 261° at 0.8 knots
    1430 (5 hours before HW) 270° at 0.7 knots
    1530 (4 hours before HW) 282° at 0.5 knots
    1430–1530 mean tidal stream is 276° at 0.6 knots

The three streams 245° at 0.7 knots, 261° at 0.8 knots and 276° at 0.6 knots should all be plotted from the 1230 fix as a 'continuation' stream (i.e. as we did on page 139).

From the end of this 'continuation' tidal stream now measure 9 miles (3 hours' run of the boat) and scribe a mark on the required track of 265°T. The direction from the end of the tidal streams to this mark on the required track will be the course to steer to counteract the streams. This, as it happens, is very close to the actual required track (course to steer 267°T). Had the streams been more individually varied then this result would not have been so close.

To counteract the leeway factor steer into the wind a bit (267°T +8° = 275°T). Now apply Variation (275°T +8°W = 283°M). Thus course to steer is 283°M.

f)   The streams have been helping the boat along. The effective speed is the distance made good over the ground (along the required track) divided by the time taken. If you measure from the 1230 fix to where the 9 miles vector cuts the track you will find this to be 11 miles and this, divided by 3, gives us 3.7 knots, which is the effective speed. But from the 1230 fix to the buoy is about 9.8 miles, so this divided by 3.7 will give the time taken to reach the buoy. This is 2.6 hours (2 hours 36 minutes). So E.T.A. is 1506 (1230 + 2 hours 36 minutes).

UNIT 11 Magnetism: Deviation

In Unit 9 Variation was described and you will recall that the amount could be found by referring to the chart.

Variation was regarded as the result of the magnetic influence which surrounds the boat and which remains unaltered regardless of the course steered, always providing that the vessel remains in the same locality. In other words if two boats were sailing in the same area then both would experience the same Variation.

Variation was applied to True courses or True bearings in order to obtain Magnetic courses or bearings. This was done by

ADDING WESTERLY VARIATION
SUBTRACTING EASTERLY VARIATION

The opposite was also applied. Magnetic courses or bearings were converted to True courses or bearings by

SUBTRACTING WESTERLY VARIATION
ADDING EASTERLY VARIATION

This information will be used consistently when Deviation is worked out.

Before we launch forth on any discussion about Deviation look at the following diagram (Fig. 11:1) and the notes underneath.

Fig. 11:1

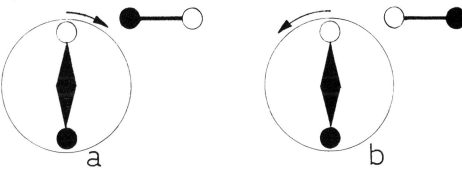

In diagram 'a' the magnetised needle is attracted by the magnet because unlike poles attract; but in diagram 'b' the needle is deviated the other way because like poles repel.

Fig. 11:2

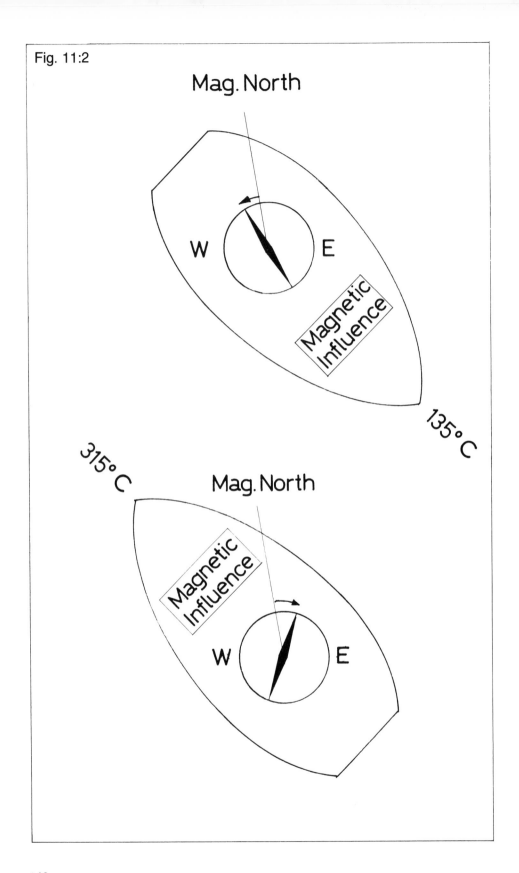

Any swing of the compass needle away from Magnetic North is called the DEVIATION and this is caused by fittings and components on a boat which have a magnetic property. Some fittings, such as many types of stainless steel, have no effect on a compass, but others, including metals which are magnetised or electrical gadgets inexpertly wired, do have a significant impact and the effect will be similar to that observed in Fig. 11:1 on page 145.

All parts of a boat which do affect the ship's main compass contribute to the overall Deviation, although it is generally assumed that there need be no, or little, Deviation on small wooden or fibreglass craft, especially if care is taken in the positioning (siting) of the compass. It should be placed as far away as possible from magnetic influences, but within easy viewing range to enable the helmsman to read it without strain. It should also be sited over the boat's centreline and, preferably, mounted high enough to be used for taking bearings. Provision for mounting it on a moveable bracket is also useful because it may then be stowed away when you are in harbour.

This overall, or total, Deviation cause may be located anywhere in the vessel; it may be in front, behind, underneath or to the side of the main compass. In Fig. 11:2 the total Deviation cause (marked as 'magnetic influence') is placed athwartships and forward of the compass but there is no significance in this choice of positioning.

Still referring to Fig. 11:2, assume that the magnetic influence which is causing the boat's Deviation is making the compass needle deviate to the westerly of the Magnetic North when the vessel is heading on a course of 135° C*. Now imagine the boat's course is altered so that she is heading 315°C and assume that the Deviation is to the easterly. This simplified illustration describes simply a process which is fundamentally scientifically complicated, but we can see that from it a basic principle emerges:

The amount and direction of the Deviation depend upon the direction of the SHIP'S HEAD.

Please read on

*C means a Compass course or bearing as registered on the ship's main compass.

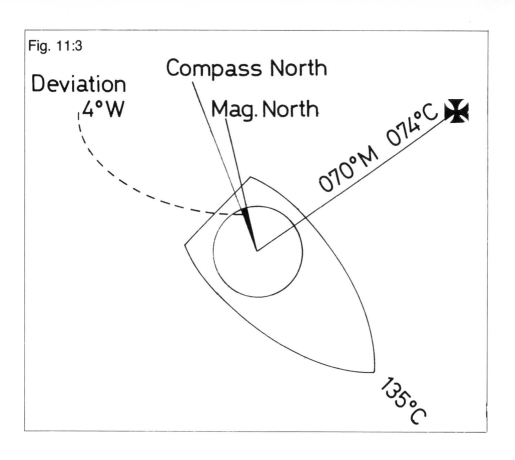

Fig. 11:3

Deviation 4°W

Compass North

Mag. North

070°M 074°C

135°C

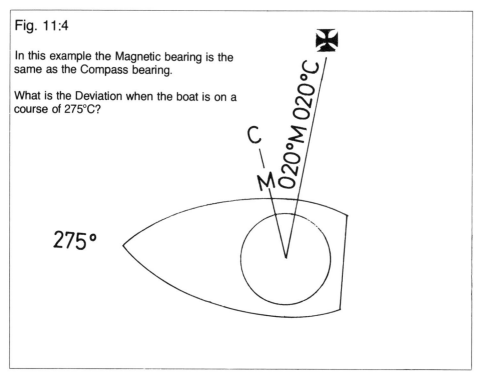

Fig. 11:4

In this example the Magnetic bearing is the same as the Compass bearing.

What is the Deviation when the boat is on a course of 275°C?

020°M 020°C

C
─
M

275°

Professional compass adjusters 'take out' as much of the Deviation as they can by placing small adjuster magnets in critical places around the compass. For example, there are small corrector magnets to be found in the compass housing itself. If you are taking possession of a new boat, or if a new compass is to be installed, then you should consider employing a trained compass adjuster to do the necessary adjustments.

But even after the error of the compass has been reduced there is often some residual Deviation left and the compass adjuster's final task is to 'swing ship' in order to find out exactly how much there is.

One way of doing this is to compare a Magnetic bearing of an object with a Compass bearing of the same mark. (This could be done by converting a known True bearing into a Magnetic bearing by taking into account the Variation; but there is no need to go into this for the purposes of this basic programme.).

Fig. 11:3 shows a boat from which it is observed that the Magnetic bearing of a church is 070°M. At the same time the main ship's compass is used to obtain a Compass bearing and this is 074°C. If the ship's head by Compass is 135°C what is the Deviation?

Well, the Deviation is the angle between the directions of Magnetic North and Compass North. In Fig. 11:3 this angle is clearly 4°. As you can see the compass needle has deviated to the westerly. So the information we want is that

When the Ship's Head is 135°C the Deviation is 4° West.

The ship is 'swung' through the various points of the compass and this technique of comparing Magnetic and Compass bearings is repeated until a 'Table of Deviations' is made up; but more of this in just a moment. Before we deal with this aspect look at Fig. 11:4 (bottom diagram) and see whether you can decide if the Deviation is east or west.

Page 151 now

Fig. 11:5

Boat's Head (Compass)	Deviation	Boat's Head (Magnetic)	Boat's Head (Compass)	Deviation	Boat's Head (Magnetic)
000 °C	2°W	358 °M	180 °C	1°E	181 °M
022½°C	3°W	019½°M	202½°C	3°E	205½°M
045 °C	4°W	041 °M	225 °C	4°E	229 °M
067½°C	6°W	061½°M	247½°C	5°E	252½°M
090 °C	4°W	086 °M	270 °C	3°E	273 °M
112½°C	3°W	109½°M	292½°C	1°E	293½°M
135 °C	1°W	134 °M	315 °C	1°W	314 °M
157½°C	0°	157½°M	337½°C	1°W	336½°M

A.

If the True course is 020°T then a westerly Variation should be added to find a magnetic course which is 026°M. Looking up under Boat's Head (Magnetic) above, 019½°M is the nearest to 026°M. Thus the Deviation for 026°M is 3°W. Still applying the same rule that a westerly Deviation should be added when going from True to Compass, we get a course of 029°C

020°T		
+6°W	Variation	
026°M		
+3°W	Deviation	
029°C	to steer	

B.

Course 310°C. Look under Boat's Head (compass): Deviation is 1°W. (315°C is nearer to 310°C).

C.

The boat's course is 330°C. Remember that the Deviation is specific to the boat's head and NOT to the bearing. Deviation is 1°W (337½°C is nearest to 330°C).

Compass bearing	075°C
Deviation	−1°W
Magnetic bearing	074°M
Variation	−5°W
True bearing	069°T

D.

Course	270°C
Deviation	+3°E
Magnetic course	273°M
Variation	+7°E
True Course	280°T

Note: You will have realised by now that, always providing you relate the Deviation to the boat's head, the method of applying it to courses or bearings is exactly the same as that used in dealing with the variation. In other words

TRUE ⟶ $\frac{-E}{+W}$ VARIATION ⟶ MAGNETIC ⟶ $\frac{-E}{+W}$ DEVIATION ⟶ COMPASS

COMPASS ⟶ $\frac{+E}{-W}$ DEVIATION ⟶ MAGNETIC ⟶ $\frac{+E}{-W}$ VARIATION ⟶ TRUE

There is no Deviation when the boat is on a compass course of 275°C. We have already considered that the deviation is the angle between the directions of Magnetic North and Compass North and since there is no angle between the two in this instance then there is no Deviation while the craft is on that particular heading.

It was established that the final task of the compass adjuster was to find out exactly how much Deviation there was in any particular boat. The end result of this procedure is a 'Table of Deviations'. Such a table is shown in Fig. 11:5. The table has three columns, 'Boat's Head (Compass)', 'Deviation' and 'Boat's Head (Magnetic)'. To find out how the system operates consider the following examples. Before you actually look at the answers on the opposite page you may care to try your hand first.

A. The skipper wants to establish a True course of 020°T. If the variation is 6° West what Compass course should he steer? (refer to box 'A' opposite.)
B. The boat is on course 310°C. What is the Deviation? (box 'B'.)
C. The skipper takes a Compass bearing of a light house which is 075°C. The boat's course is 330°C. Variation is 5°West. What is the True bearing of the light? (Box 'C'.)
D. The craft is steering a course of 270°C. Variation is 7°East. What is the True course? (Box 'D'.)

Now do this example, but if you haven't already done so read the footnote on page 150.
At 1145 on 12 April 1976 the yacht is on passage steering a course of 245°C. The skipper, using a steering compass mounted on the cabin top, takes a compass bearing of a tower which is 000°C. Variation is 5° East. What is the True bearing of the tower?

True bearing is 003°T . . . page 152
True bearing is 010°T . . . page 153

|X| *003T° is wrong*

Did you look up the compass bearing of 000°C in the 'Table of Deviations'? If you did then you would have arrived at the wrong answer.

The Deviation is always related to the boat's head and in this example this was 245°C. So the full working would be as follows.

Compass bearing	000°C
Deviation (boat's head is 245°C; 247½°C is nearest)	+5° East
Magnetic bearing	005°M
Variation	+5° East
True bearing	010°T

Another way in which you may have been wrong is in applying Deviation and/or the Variation wrongly. It may help to remember the word CADET. It means Compass ADd East True or more fully, COMPASS TO TRUE ADD EAST. This is a starting point from which you can work out the other 'rules' of how to apply Variation and Deviation. That is,

COMPASS TO TRUE ADD EAST (AND SUBTRACT WEST)
TRUE TO COMPASS SUBTRACT EAST (AND ADD WEST)

To reinforce the idea look at the following aid to memory:

COMPASS apply Deviation $^{+E}_{-W}$ MAGNETIC apply Variation $^{+E}_{-W}$ TRUE

$\longrightarrow$

TRUE apply Variation $^{-E}_{+W}$ MAGNETIC apply Deviation $^{-E}_{+W}$ COMPASS

$\longrightarrow$

Return to page 151 and re-check examples A, B, C and D

Summary

a) Deviation is caused by various fittings and components installed on the boat affecting the compass.

b) The amount and direction of the Deviation depends upon the direction of the ship's head.

c) Deviation is the angle between Magnetic North and Compass North.

d) Deviation is found by a comparison of Compass bearings with Magnetic bearings.

e) A 'Table of Deviations' is compiled.

f) Well-adjusted compasses on small wooden or fibreglass craft should have no, or at most very little, Deviation.

Exercise 11

For this exercise use the 'Table of Deviations' on page 150 and, where necessary, the Tide Tables on page 94. It is assumed throughout the exercise that bearings are taken with the main steering compass.

a) 23 September 1975
   At 1715 auxiliary yacht *Caribou of Burnham* is sailing in the vicinity of 'The Bellows' just to the southerly of Dodman Point. The course is 243°C and during the past hour the speed was estimated at 3.5 knots. The log reads 20.1 and the wind is N force 3. There is no leeway.
   LHE Nare Head 269°C RHE Dodman Point 035°C
   Caerhay's Castle 337°C
   What is the 1715 fix?

b) If the speed and course are maintained what would be the 1815 DR Pos. and the 1815 EP?

c) At 1815 the wind backs and freshens to NW force 4. The leeway is 10° and the log is 24.6
   LHE Nare Head 320°C LHE Zone Point 248°C
   Gerrans Church 276°C
   What is the 1815 fix?

d) Speed now estimated at 4.5 knots.
   What would be the Compass course to steer to MAKE GOOD a required track of 238°T during the period from 1815 to 1915?
   (Here you should –
      plot required track
      estimate tidal streams
      lay-off a True course to counteract streams
      alter course to counteract leeway effect
      finally apply Variation and Deviation.)

Answers on the next page (overleaf)

Answers: Exercise 11

a) The course is 243°C, therefore Deviation is 5°E. Since the boat's head is the critical factor the Deviation which will apply to the two bearings is 5°E.
LHE Nare Head 269°C Deviation 5°E 274°M Variation 9°W 265°T
RHE Dodman Point 035°C Deviation 5°E 040°M Variation 9°W 031°T
Caerhays Castle 337°C Deviation 5°E 342°M Variation 9°W 333°T
1715 fix 50°12'.1N   04°48'.8W.

b) Course 243°C Deviation 5°E Course 248°M Variation 9°W Course 239°T
1815 DR Pos. 50°10'.3N   04°53'.4W.
HW time 23 September 1975 is 1915 G.M.T. (2015 B.S.T.). We are at Springs. Tidal diamond ⟨E⟩ is used.
Streams 1715 (3 hours before HW) to 1815 (2 hours before HW):
3 hours before HW 077° 0.2 knots
2 hours before HW 037° 0.4 knots
Mean stream 1715–1815 is 057° at 0.3 knots
1815 EP 50°10'.5N   04°53'W.

c) The yacht is still on course 243°C so Deviation is still 5°E.
LHE Nare Head 320°C Deviation 5°E 325°M Variation 9°W 316°T
LHE Zone Point 248°C Deviation 5°E 253°M Variation 9°W 244°T
Gerrans Church 276°C Deviation 5°E 281°M Variation 9°W 272°T
1815 fix 50°10'.6N   04°53'.5W.

d) Tidal streams (still using ⟨E⟩):
1815 (2 hours before HW) 037° 0.4knots
1915 (1 hour before HW) 042° 0.5 knots
Mean stream 1815 to 1915 is about 040° at 0.5 knots
The True course to counteract the streams and make good the required track of 238°T is 236°T. Since the yacht is on the starboard tack (i.e. wind is hitting the starboard side) the 10° leeway will have to be added to the course of 236°T in order that the leeway may be counteracted. The course to steer to counteract both streams and leeway is therefore 246°T (236° + 10°). Now the Variation should be applied. The Magnetic course is 255°M (246° + 9°). If you refer to the 'Table of Deviations' under Boat's Head (Magnetic) then the Deviation for 255°M can be found. This is 5°E. Apply this to the Magnetic course of 255°M (−5°) and the Compass course to steer finally comes out as 250°C.

UNIT 12 Tidal Levels

There isn't much point in knowing how to plot a safe passage only to find that, on arriving at your destination, you cannot take your boat into harbour because there isn't enough water to float her.

Many sailors, particularly those who sail craft which are deep keel vessels, need to know how to find the level of the tides in order to operate success-fully around their coastal areas.

This unit teaches you a method of calculating tidal levels. Note however that storms and other meteorological occurrences can upset tidal predicti-ons.

The Admiralty Tide Tables, Vol. 1, which is the reference we have used in this programme whenever tidal influences have been discussed, contains two main parts, one dealing with the Standard ports and the other concerned with the Secondary ports.

The Secondary port is no less important than the Standard port. The system is that information in great detail is provided about the Standard port. This information then serves as a basis for deciding what happens to the tidal pattern at ports which are close to the Standard port. You will see in this and the next unit how the system works, and Fig. 12:1 gives an idea of the way the Secondary ports are clustered about the Standard port. This unit deals with the Standard ports.

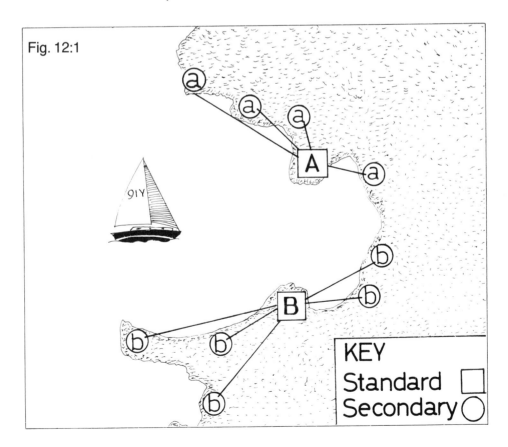

Fig. 12:1

KEY
Standard □
Secondary ○

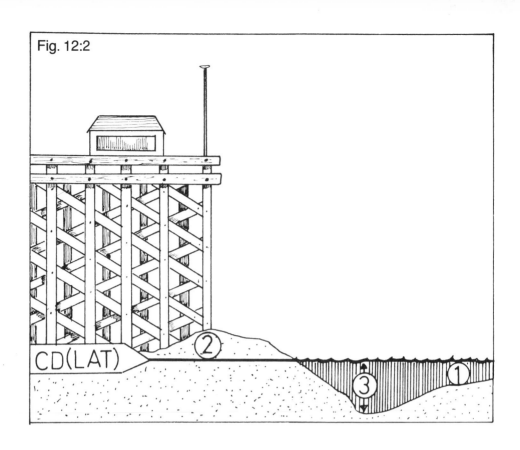

Fig. 12:2

CD(LAT)

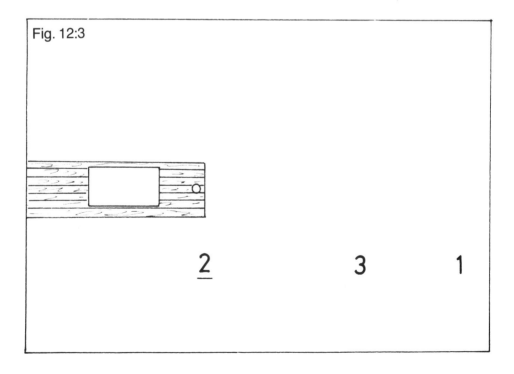

Fig. 12:3

2   3   1

You will recall that the tides are governed by the positions of the moon and the sun, and also that such events as Springs and Neap tides occur (page 96, Figs. 7:5, 7:6, 7:7).

Because of the movements of the heavenly bodies it was evident that the levels of the sea varied from day to day. Spring HW levels were higher than they were at Neaps. Spring LW levels are also lower than Neap LW levels (you will have seen this when studying the Tide Tables on page 94).

There are occasions when the tidal levels rise far more than at any other normal time; they could be described as reaching 'astronomical' levels. On such instances we can get what are referred to as the Highest Astronomical Tides. At the lower end of the scale there can occur what is called the LOWEST ASTRONOMICAL TIDE, and this is the lowest level to which the tide will fall under any combination of astronomical conditions and where average meteorological conditions prevail. A note of caution here – the Lowest Astronomical Tide (LAT) is not the lowest level which the tide may ever reach because storm surges may occasionally make the level fall even lower! However, the LAT will not occur every year so the tide level will very rarely fall below it, certainly not frequently enough for the small boat sailor to concern himself about it.

In Fig. 12:2 a side-on view of a pier is shown with a bumpy sea bed underneath it. The LAT level is drawn. This level we may now regard as a level of reference and give it its common name of CHART DATUM.* This sounds a little complicated but it isn't really. All it means is that all the levels concerning tides are referred to Chart Datum (CD). Fig. 12:3 shows how the sea area depicted in Fig. 12:2 would be drawn when illustrated on a chart. Notice that where the CD is below the sea bed (i.e. where the seabed dries) the level is given as a figure with a line underneath it. So 2 means that at that point the sea bed dries 2 metres above CD.

Please look at the practice chart and attempt to answer the following questions.

Does the sea bed dry out to a height of 2.4 metres above CD in position 50°20′.5N   04°41′.5W?

Page 159

---

*The established levels of datums at Standard ports vary widely. However, LAT is now accepted as the level to which datum is gradually being adjusted.

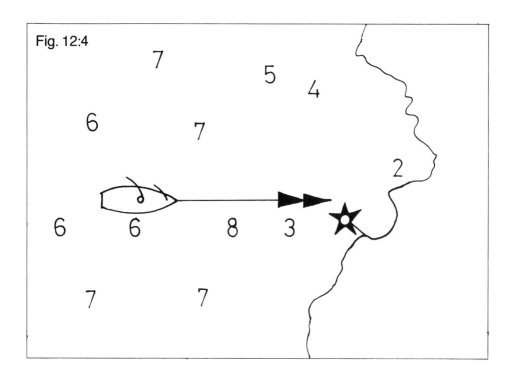

Fig. 12:4

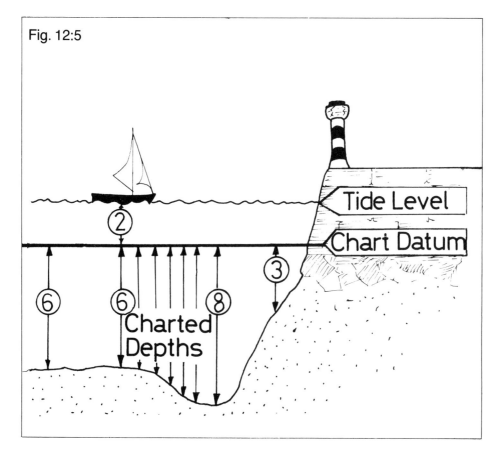

Fig. 12:5

At Par Sands the figure given is 2₄ which means that at that position the sea bed does dry out at 2.4 metres.

Throughout the programme we have realised that the numbers on the chart are measurements of the depth of the water. These figures are called CHARTED DEPTHS.

In Fig. 12:4 a boat is sailing along a track and she is seen to be moving over a charted depth of 6 metres. Now suppose the skipper switches on the echo sounder (which is a gadget for recording the depth of the water) and gets a reading of, say, 8 metres. This seems in error because the two figures do not tally. The reason for this is given in the next diagram.

In Fig. 12:5 we see a section (side-on) view of what the sea bed would look like directly beneath the vessel's track. Now we can see that the Charted Depths are measured from the sea bed to CHART DATUM.

Notice also that the TIDAL LEVEL, as in Fig. 12:5, is measured from Chart Datum to the actual level of the sea.

So the 8 metres depth may now be regarded as a combination of the height above (2 metres) and the depth below (6 metres) Chart Datum (CD).

Quite a good way of checking your position is to compare the charted depth with the reading you get on the echo-sounder or, if you have one, a lead-line, taking into account the tidal level at the time. If there is a particular feature of the sea bed, such as a sudden trough or ridge, which is easily identified by the boat's sounding equipment, it can be used to get added information about your position. You can compare the soundings over which your craft tracks with the chart information, and obtain some welcome evidence which enables you to get a more reliable position. This is most useful when other information is unreliable or unobtainable, for example in thick fog when bearings on known navigational marks are impossible to take, or when the D/F set has failed. In fog it is most important to steer accurate compass courses and be more than usually careful about plotting a regular EP, keeping the log written up and so on, since in coastal waters there is the added danger of collision to contend with.

A boat is cruising over an area which is charted as 6 metres but the echo sounder records a depth of 9 metres. How much water is above CD?

Tidal level is 3 metres . . . *page 163*
Tidal level is 15 metres . . . *page 161*

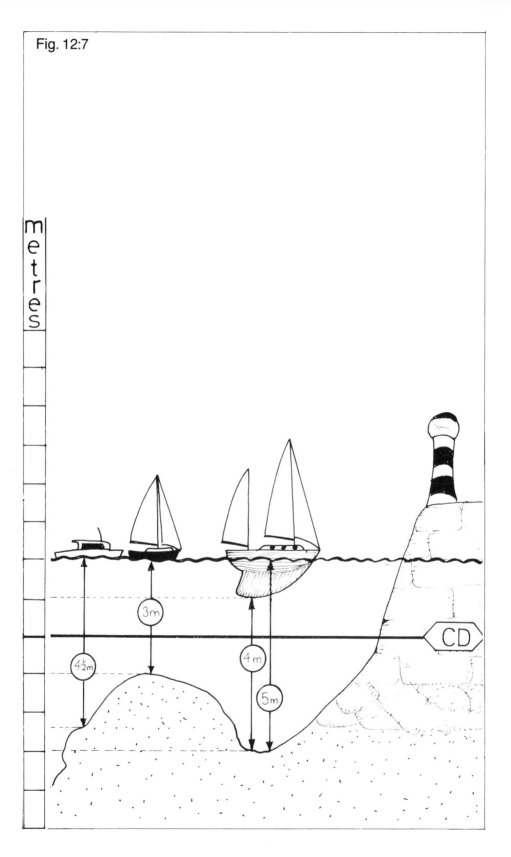

Fig. 12:7

metres

3m

4½m

4 m

5m

CD

The total depth of water is 9m because that is the depth which the echo sounder records. The depth could not possibly be 15m under the circumstances. Now the charted depth (i.e. the depth from the sea bed to Chart Datum) is given as 6m. The depth of sea above Chart Datum must therefore be 3m. The diagram below (Fig. 12:6) illustrates the situation.

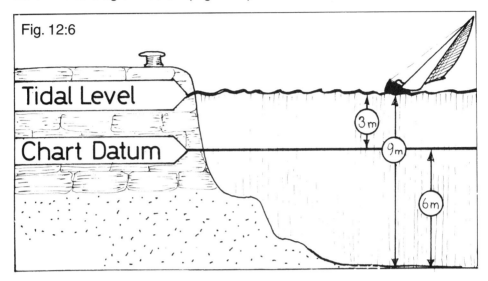

Fig. 12:6

Tidal Level

Chart Datum

If you also refer to Fig. 12:7 on the opposite page several examples of depths as they relate to Chart Datum are pictured. The small powered launch is over a patch which would be charted as $2\frac{1}{2}$m but the overall depth of water under her would be $4\frac{1}{2}$m because the $2\frac{1}{2}$ charted depth refers to a measurement which is between the sea bed and Chart Datum.

The sloop (1 mast) is over a charted depth which would be given as 1m on the chart and the ketch (2 masts) is over a charted depth of 3m BUT, because her draft (depth of vessel beneath the sea level) is 1m, there is only 4m of water under her keel and not 5m as might have been anticipated. This measure of a vessel's draft should always be reckoned with in estimating suitable clearance depths when entering or leaving small harbours.

Have another look at page 159 and then move on

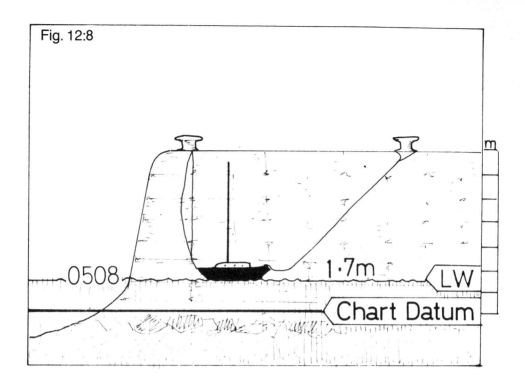

Fig. 12:8

0508   1·7m   LW

Chart Datum

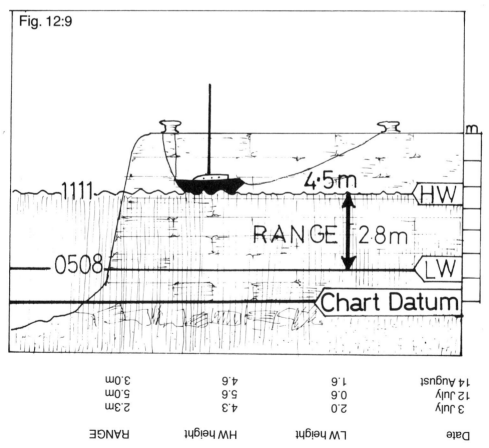

Fig. 12:9

1111   4·5m   HW

RANGE 2·8m

0508   LW

Chart Datum

Date	LW height	HW height	RANGE
3 July	2.0	4.3	2.3m
12 July	0.6	5.6	5.0m
14 August	1.6	4.6	3.0m

162

Our main concern at this moment is to learn how to predict the height of tide ABOVE CD; in other words, how do we calculate how much water there is above CD at any particular time? Below is an extract printed from Fig. 7:3 on page 94.

1 July 1975	0408 (G.M.T.)	0508 (B.S.T.)	1.7m
	1011 (G.M.T.)	1111 (B.S.T.)	4.5m
	1623 (G.M.T.)	1723 (B.S.T.)	1.9m
	2229 (G.M.T.)	2329 (B.S.T.)	4.6m

In the Admiralty Tide Tables all heights are given as 'heights above CD'. Look at Fig. 12:8. There you see the harbour wall, alongside which is moored a boat. She is floating at the level of Low Water which is 1.7m. It is plainly seen that the level of LW is 1.7m above the CD line.

Similarly in Fig. 12:9 the yacht is now floating at HW level, which is 4.5m.

The difference between the LW and HW levels is called the RANGE and in the diagram this is 2.8m (4.5m–1.7m.)

What are the Ranges of tide on the following days?

3 July 1975 (am)

12 July 1975 (pm)

14 August 1975 (pm)

(The answers are upside down on the opposite page)

Having discovered the Range that applies over a particular duration, we then have to find out where within the Range the tidal level will be at a particular time.

The tidal level does not change at a consistent rate throughout the duration. For instance, the amount of fall in the first hour after HW would not be the same as the amount of fall in the third hour after HW. We therefore have to consult a graph from which we can find out what proportion of the range above LW height will be covered at any specified time before or after HW. This is expressed in the graph as a 'factor' – the proportion of the whole range expressed as a decimal. The principle of the graph is shown in the following diagram.

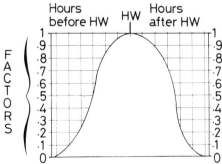

LW height is represented by zero and HW height by 1.

Page 165 please

(From the Admiralty Tide Tables, Vol. 1, 1975, Part I. Crown copyright. Reproduced with the permission of The Hydrographer of the Navy.

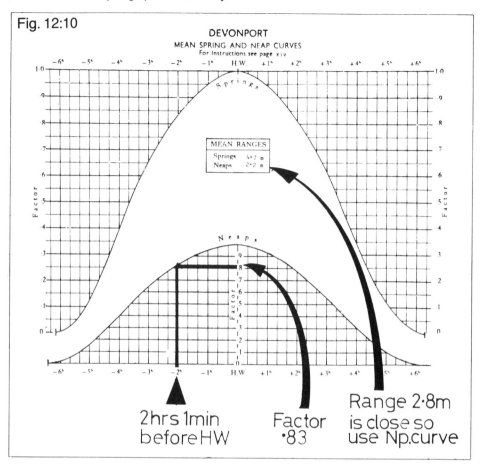

Fig. 12:10

DEVONPORT

MEAN SPRING AND NEAP CURVES
For Instructions see page xiv

MEAN RANGES
Springs 4·7 m
Neaps   2·2 m

2hrs 1min
before HW

Factor
·83

Range 2·8m
is close so
use Np.curve

(These graphs are used in conjunction with the tidal information given in the A.T.T.s. This particular graph, Devonport, relates to Fig. 7:3, page 94)

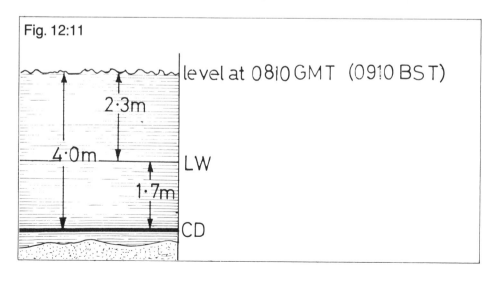

Fig. 12:11

level at 0810 GMT (0910 BST)

2·3m

4·0m   LW

1·7m

CD

In Fig. 12:10 two graphs are shown, one for Springs and one for Neaps.
The actual tidal level ABOVE CHART DATUM for any time of the day may be predicted as follows:
1.   Find the level above LW height
2.   Add this level to the LW height.

We can use this example to follow the way the calculations are done:
What is the predicted height of tide above Chart Datum at Devonport on 1 July 1975 at 0910 B.S.T.? (We shall use G.M.T. throughout and convert back to B.S.T. at the end.)

To answer this we need the RANGE, the LW height and the amount of time before or after HW.
Working from the Tide Tables (page 94) we obtain the following:

LW time	0408		2h. 1 min	LW height 1.7m		RANGE IS
		▶ 0810	before HW		▶	2.8m
HW time	1011			HW height 4.5m		

The Range of 2.8m is significantly closer to the Mean Neap Range than to the Mean Spring Range (this information is printed in the box in the centre of the graphs), so we use the Neap curve.
Using the Neap curve and entering the graph 2 hours 1 minute before (-2 hours 1 minute) read up to where you meet the actual curve, then across to where it reads 'Factor'. The factor is .83. Multiply the Range by the factor and this will give us the height of tide above LW at 0810 G.M.T. (0910 B.S.T.).

| RANGE | | FACTOR | | Height above LW height |
| 2.8 | × | .83 | = | 2.3m |

In order to find the level of the tide ABOVE CD then we must add 2.3m to the LW height, which is 1.7m. The answer is $2.3 + 1.7 = 4.0$m. Please look at Fig. 12:11 to get a picture of the whole situation.
The final part of this unit involves finding out at what time the tidal level will be at a given height above CD.
What is the predicted time after am High Water at Devonport by which the tide will have fallen to 3m above CD on 4 July 1975?

HW time 0033 HW height 4.3m ⎫
HW time 0702 LW height 2.0m ⎭   Range 2.3m $(4.3 - 2.0)$ This is a Neap Range

To find out the Factor (in order to read off the graph the time – or +HW) we divide the height above LW by the Range. The height above LW is the height required minus LW height $(3.0m - 2.0m = 1.0m)$.

$$\frac{\text{Height above LW}}{\text{Range}} = \text{Factor } \frac{1.0}{2.3} = .43$$

Referring to the graph (Neaps curve) we get a time 3 hours 30 minutes after HW (+3 hours 30 minutes) corresponding with the factor .43. Adding this to HW time we get 0403 G.M.T. (0503 B.S.T.) (HW time 0033 + 3 hours 30 minutes).

Carry on to the next page (166)

Here are two more examples similar to the ones you have been looking at.
With them are diagrams which may help to clarify matters.

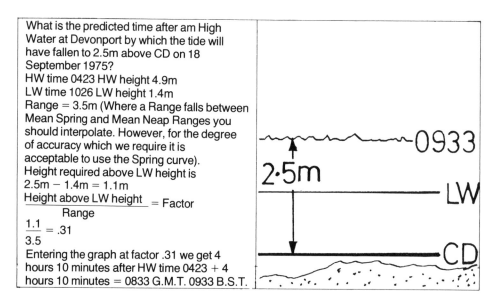

What will be the height of the tide above CD on 12 July 1975 at 1300 B.S.T. (Devonport)?
HW time 0810 HW height 5.3m
LW time 1404 LW height 0.6m
Range = 4.7m (so use Spring curve)
1300 B.S.T. (1200 G.M.T.) is 3 hours 50 minutes after HW (+3 hours 50 minutes)
Factor .39
Range × Factor = Height above LW
4.7   .39   1.8m

1.8m + 0.6m (LW height) = 2.4m

What is the predicted time after am High Water at Devonport by which the tide will have fallen to 2.5m above CD on 18 September 1975?
HW time 0423 HW height 4.9m
LW time 1026 LW height 1.4m
Range = 3.5m (Where a Range falls between Mean Spring and Mean Neap Ranges you should interpolate. However, for the degree of accuracy which we require it is acceptable to use the Spring curve).
Height required above LW height is
2.5m − 1.4m = 1.1m
$\dfrac{\text{Height above LW height}}{\text{Range}}$ = Factor
$\dfrac{1.1}{3.5}$ = .31
Entering the graph at factor .31 we get 4 hours 10 minutes after HW time 0423 + 4 hours 10 minutes = 0833 G.M.T. 0933 B.S.T.

You should now do the following. Also attempt to draw diagrams illustrating the answer.
A. What will be the height of the tide above CD at Devonport 7 July 1975 at 0600 B.S.T.?
b. What is the predicted time after am High Water at Devonport by which the tide will have fallen to 3m above CD on 4 August 1975?

Move on to page 168 for the answers

Summary

a) The Admiralty Tide Tables, Vol 1., deals with Standard and Secondary ports.
b) The Lowest Astronomical Tide is the level of reference which is often used as Chart Datum.
c) Charted depths are measurements from the sea bed to Chart Datum.
d) All tidal predictions are given as heights above Chart Datum.
e) Tidal levels are frequently influenced by storm surges.
f) Graphs are used to calculate tidal levels.

Exercise 12

a) What is the height of tide above CD at 1815 B.S.T. at Devonport 12 July 1975?
b) What is the predicted time before pm High Water at Devonport by which the tide will have reached 3m above CD on 14 August 1975?

Answers below

Answers: Exercise 12

a) 1815 B.S.T. (1715 G.M.T.)
LW time 1404   LW height 0.6
HW time 2024   HW height 5.6
Range = 5.0m
Interval −3 hours 09 minutes
Factor (use Spring curve) .63
5.0 × .63 = 3.15m height above LW height
3.2 + 0.6 = 3.8m above CD at 1815 B.S.T.

b) LW time 1644   LW height 1.6
HW time 2301   HW height 4.6
Range 3.0m (use Neap curve)
Height required above LW height is
3.0 − 1.6 = 1.4m
$\frac{1.4}{3.0}$ = Factor .47
Interval −3 hours 50 minutes
2301 − 3 hours 50 minutes is 1911 G.M.T. (2011 B.S.T.)

Here are the answers to the problems on page 166 with associated diagrams. After you have checked them out return to page 167.

What will be the height of the tide above CD at Devonport on 7 July 1975 at 0600 B.S.T.? (Note: if Range is not significantly closer to Springs or Neaps, use the Springs curve).
HW time 0349 HW height 4.7m
LW time 1007 LW height 1.4m
Range = 3.3m (use Spring curve)
0600 B.S.T. (0500 G.M.T.) is 1 hour 11 minutes after HW (+ 1 hour 11 minutes)
Factor .93
Range × Factor = Height above LW
  3.3   .93   3.1m
Height above LW 3.1m + LW height 1.4 = 4.5m

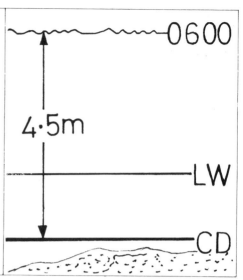

What is the predicted time after am High Water at Devonport by which the tide will have fallen to 3m above CD on 4 August 1975?
HW time 0209 HW height 4.4m
LW time 0837 LW height 1.9m
Range = 2.5m (use Neap curve)
Height required above LW height is
3m − 1.9m = 1.1m
$\dfrac{\text{Height above LW height}}{\text{Range}}$ = Factor

$\dfrac{1.1}{2.5}$ = .44

From graph, reading factor .44 we get 3 hours 24 minutes after HW time.
0209 + 3 hours 24 minutes = 0533 G.M.T.
0633 B.S.T.

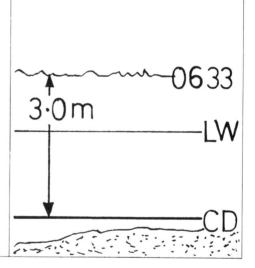

UNIT 13 Secondary Ports

This is the final unit of the programme and you may find that it is the most tedious. But stick with it and master it because in a way it is possibly the most important of all.

Here we discuss how to enter and leave shallow water harbours. Many small craft sailors appear to spend their sailing lives doing just this. Along many stretches of coastline such as from Land's End north to Holyhead, there are surprisingly few deep-water havens where a fin keel yacht may be taken at any time of the day or night without the need for 'taking the ground'.

Learn this unit well and the chances are you may be able to get to work on Monday morning instead of having to wait hours for the next favourable tide to re-float you!

Page 171 now

Fig. 13:1

(From Admiralty Tide Tables, Vol. 1, 1975, Part II. Crown copyright. Reproduced with the permission of The Hydrographer of the Navy)

No.	PLACE	POSITION		TIMES AT STANDARD PORT				HEIGHTS (IN METRES) AT STANDARD PORT			
	STANDARD PORT	Lat. N.	Long. W.	High Water at		Low Water at		MHWS	MHWN	MLWN	MLWS
				0000 and 1200	0600 and 1800	0000 and 1200	0600 and 1800				
14	DEVONPORT	(see page 2)						5·5	4·4	2·2	0·8
	SECONDARY PORTS			TIME DIFFERENCES				HEIGHT DIFFERENCES			
				(Zone G.M.T.)							
	Scilly Isles										
1	St. Mary's	49 55	6 19	−0030	−0110	−0100	−0020	+0·2	−0·1	−0·2	−0·1
2	Penzance (Newlyn)	50 06	5 33	−0040	−0105	−0045	−0020	+0·1	0·0	−0·2	0·0
2a	Porthleven	50 05	5 19	−0045	−0105	−0035	−0025	0·0	−0·1	−0·2	0·0
3	Lizard Point	49 57	5 12	−0045	−0055	−0040	−0030	−0·2	−0·2	−0·3	−0·2
4	Coverack	50 01	5 05	−0030	−0040	−0020	−0010	−0·2	−0·2	−0·3	−0·2
4a	Helford River (Entrance)	50 05	5 05	−0030	−0035	−0015	−0010	−0·2	−0·2	−0·3	−0·2
	River Fal										
5	Falmouth	50 09	5 03	−0030	−0030	−0010	−0010	−0·2	−0·2	−0·3	−0·2
5a	Truro	50 16	5 03	−0020	−0025	★	★	−0·2	−0·2	★	★
7	Mevagissey	50 16	4 47	−0010	−0015	−0005	+0005	−0·1	−0·1	−0·2	−0·1
8	Fowey	50 20	4 38	−0010	−0015	−0010	−0005	−0·1	−0·1	−0·2	−0·2
11	Looe	50 21	4 27	−0010	−0010	−0005	−0005	−0·1	−0·2	−0·2	−0·2
12	Whitesand Bay	50 20	4 15	0000	0000	0000	0000	0·0	+0·1	−0·1	+0·2
13	Plymouth (Breakwater)	50 20	4 09	−0006	−0006	−0006	−0006	0·0	0·0	◊	◊

★ Dries out at low water.   No data.

† Between Dartmouth and Portland the tidal curve gradually becomes more and more distorted, especially on the rising tide; the rise is relatively fast for the first hour after low water and there is then a noticeable slackening in the rate of rise for the next 1½ hours, after which the rapid rate of rise is resumed. There is often a "stand" at high water which, while not very noticeable at Dartmouth, lasts for about an hour at Torquay and for 1½ hours at Lyme Regis.

‡ Double low waters occur between Portland and Lulworth Cove. Data for Lulworth refer to the first low water.

HEIGHTS IN METRES

Fig. 13:2

Find the HW and LW times and heights (above CD) Helford River 13 August (pm)

Devonport HW time	2213 (G.M.T.)	LW time	1554 (G.M.T.)
Helford difference	−0032	Helford difference	−0012
Helford HW time	2141 (G.M.T.)	Helford LW time	1542 (G.M.T.)
	2241 (B.S.T.)		1642 (B.S.T.)

(In this instance both HW and LW times are somewhere between the times in the columns above. For example, the HW time 2213 occurs about two-thirds along the duration 1800–0000. Two-thirds of the difference between −0030 and −0035 is about 3 minutes. The same principles of interpolation also apply to LW times.)

Devonport HW height	5.0	Devonport LW height	1.2
Helford difference	−0.2	Helford difference	−0.2
Helford HW height	4.8m	Helford LW height	1.0m

(Where heights are concerned if they fall between the Mean Springs and Mean Neaps values then again you should interpolate.)

What are the HW and LW times and heights (above CD) at Porthleven on 7 July (pm)?

Page 173 now

Fig. 13:1 is a sample of a page out of the A.T.T. (Part II) which deals with Secondary ports.

The times and heights of tides at Standard ports differ from those at the associated Secondary ports. To show the method of working the following question will be answered:

What are the times and heights of LW and HW (above CD) at Fowey on the morning of 3 July 1975?

First we need information about the related Standard port times.

Devonport information (from page 94):

HW time 1208 (G.M.T.) LW time 0552 (G.M.T.). Now find out which time duration our HW time of 1208 is in: it is in 1200–1800 (encircled in Fig. 13:1). Also decide where along that duration it is. Then, having found the column, look down until the time differences at Fowey are seen. The following diagram sums it up:

The HW time in question falls about here on the Time and Difference scale, so call the HW Time Difference at Fowey −10 minutes. Therefore the Fowey HW time is as follows:

Devonport HW time	1208 (G.M.T.)
Fowey difference	−0010
Fowey HW time	1158 (G.M.T.) which is 1258 (B.S.T.)

By using the same method of applying differences in time, we can obtain the LW time at Fowey as follows:

Devonport LW time	0552 (G.M.T.)
Fowey difference	−0005
Fowey LW time	0547 (G.M.T.) which is 0647 (B.S.T.)

In order to find the Fowey heights at LW and HW the columns referring to 'Height Differences' should be consulted. The following diagram, which uses data selected from Fig. 13:1, sums up the method:

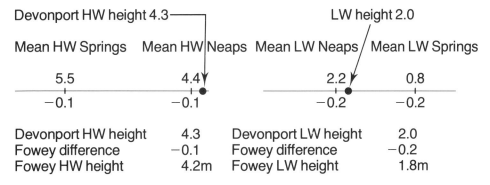

Devonport HW height	4.3	Devonport LW height	2.0
Fowey difference	−0.1	Fowey difference	−0.2
Fowey HW height	4.2m	Fowey LW height	1.8m

Study the example in Fig. 13:2 and answer the question at the foot of it.

Fig. 13:3

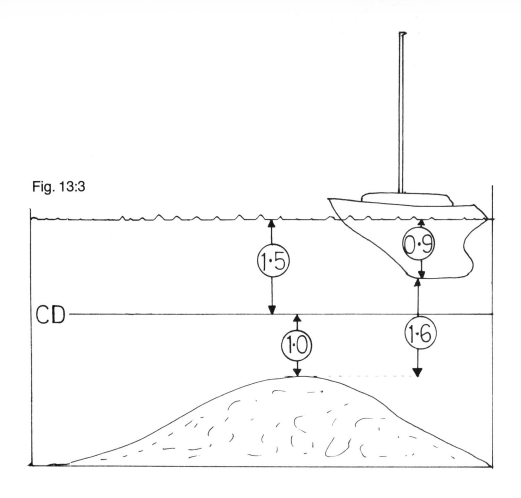

Fig. 13:4

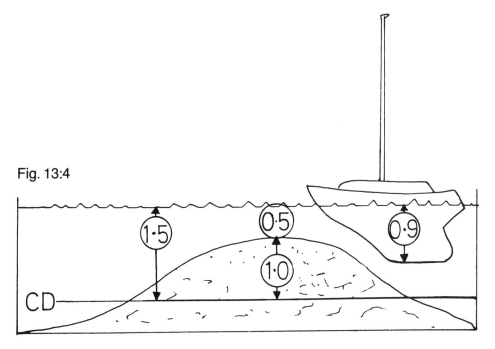

Here is the answer in full:

7 July 1975

Devonport HW time	1618 (G.M.T.)	Devonport LW time	2235 (G.M.T.)
Porthleven difference	−0058	Porthleven difference	−0032
Porthleven HW time	1520 (G.M.T.)	Porthleven LW time	2203 (G.M.T.)
	1620 (B.S.T.)		2303 (B.S.T.)

Devonport HW height	5.0	Devonport LW height	1.3
Porthleven difference	0.0	Porthleven difference	−0.1
Porthleven HW height	5.0m	Porthleven LW height	1.2m

Before we round off this very small unit there is just one consideration which we would be wise to look into.

Having discovered that the sea bed is not a convenient uniform flatness but that it is in fact very often extremely uneven, we should consider the problem of taking a boat into a harbour which has very limited depth of water at certain times during the day. Take as an example the illustration in Fig. 13:3. There you can see a 'bar' (that spot where the sand piles up into a heap which is often situated at the entrance to a harbour) and in this instance CD is above the sea bed. That means there will usually always be 1.0m height of water above the bed always providing there are no abnormal meteorological conditions or that there isn't a very steep wave system prevailing at the time which would cause problems. The actual tidal level (i.e. height ABOVE CD) is 1.5m. Now if a yacht with a draft of, say, 0.9m sails over that bar there will be a total clearance of 1.6m. The situation could be written down as follows:

Tidal level	1.5m
CD at bar	+1.0m
Total depth	2.5m
Draft	−0.9m
Clearance	1.6m

Notice that another way of showing that CD is above the sea bed, or if you like that there is always water above the sea bed, is to say that CD is +1.0m. But if the sea bed is above CD, then it would sometimes be written as −1.0m.

Now refer to Fig. 13:4, where the sea bed is above CD at the bar. In this case we can write down the situation like this:

Tidal level	1.5m
CD at bar	−1.0m
Total depth	0.5m
Draft	−0.9m – NO CLEARANCE

Assume that CD at a port was −0.5m at the quay. What is the minimum depth of water required above CD which would allow a yacht with a draft of 0.4m to float alongside the quay?

0.9m . . . *page 174*
0.1m . . . *page 175*

✓ Right

This is the last new piece of learning to be dealt with in this programme. As you will see, incorporating this in what we have learnt previously is relatively simple. Work through an example.

> At 1600 a yacht (draft 0.8m) is sailing just off Mevagissey. The skipper wishes to put into the inner harbour. If the CD is given as −1.2 metres at the centre of the inner harbour what is the earliest time the yacht could get in?

The CD is 1.2m BELOW the sea bed, so at least 2.0m is needed above CD (1.2 + 0.8). Next we convert the data for the Standard port (which is Devonport) into data for the Secondary port. (Use Fig. 7:3 on page 94, Fig. 13:1 on page 170 and Fig. 12:10 on page 164.)

Devonport HW time	2133 (G.M.T.)	Devonport LW time	1511 (G.M.T.)
Mevagissey difference	−0013	Mevagissey difference	0000
Mevagissey HW time	2120 (G.M.T.)	Mevagissey LW time	1511 (G.M.T.)
	2220 (B.S.T.)		1611 (B.S.T.)

Devonport HW height	5.3	Devonport LW height	0.8
Mevagissey difference	−0.1	Mevagissey difference	−0.1
Mevagissey HW height	5.2m	Mevagissey LW height	0.7

Mevagissey Range = 4.5m (5.2 − 0.7.)

If 2.0m is needed (above CD) then at least 1.3m is needed above LW (which is 0.7m). Therefore 1.3m of the total Range of 4.5m is required in order to float the craft into the inner harbour.

There is just one thing left to do before we use the graph on page 164 to find the necessary information, and that is to find out what the Mean Ranges are at Mevagissey so that we can compare our Range above (4.5m) with them. By doing that we can then enter the graph at the right curve, Springs or Neaps. The following information comes from Fig. 13:1 on page 170. Be sure to find it and follow the reasoning.

	MHWS	MHWN	MLWN	MLWS
DEVONPORT heights	5.5	4.4	2.2	0.8
MEVAGISSEY differences	−0.1	−0.1	−0.2	−0.1
MEVAGISSEY heights	5.4	4.3	2.0	0.7

MEVAGISSEY MEAN RANGES Mean Spring Range   Mean Neap Range
                                      4.7   (5.4 − 0.7)   2.3   (4.3 − 2.0)

Now we need to find the Factor from the graph. If you recall we used the following formula: $\dfrac{\text{Height required above LW height}}{\text{Range}} = \text{Factor}$

Thus factor = $\dfrac{1.3}{4.5}$ = .29

Now looking up the Spring curve (because the Mevagissey 12 August 1975 Range of 4.5 is significantly close to the Mevagissey Mean Spring Range of 4.7), we can see that the time when there will be 1.3m above LW height is about 4 hours 20 minutes before HW time of 2120. This is 1700 G.M.T. Add 1 hour to get B.S.T. and we arrive at the time of 1800 B.S.T. The skipper has to wait two hours before he can get in.   *Please go to page 176*

Since the CD is 0.5m BELOW the sea bed at the quay then this depth is required in addition to the amount needed to float the craft. Fig. 13:5 below outlines the situation. You should study this drawing and then refer to the page opposite (174).

Fig. 13:5

Summary

a) By using the information relating to Standard ports and applying differences of heights and times associated at the Secondary ports, all necessary information regarding tides at these Secondary ports may be found.

b) The draft of a vessel must be taken into consideration when entering or leaving shallow waters.

Exercise 13

(Here are two questions. The first sets the problem of finding the total depth of water given a certain time. The second asks you to predict a time when a specified depth is required).

1. What is the TOTAL DEPTH of water at Looe on 1 August 1975 at noon? (CD −0.3m.)

2. What is the predicted time before pm High Water at Fowey by which the TOTAL DEPTH of water will be 8.0m on 10 August 1975? (CD is +6.1m in the channel).

The answers follow the Test Piece on page 178.

After you have done these try the last Test Piece on the next page

FINAL TEST PIECE

This problem involves a deep-keel yacht (draft 1.8m) with auxiliary power. She is on passage from Plymouth to Looe. Use all the standard references such as the A.T.T. (Figs. 7:3 and 13:1). The principles needed to work out the exercise are those which have been taught in the programme – indeed there is a bit of everything embodied within this Test Piece. Remember that all Magnetic courses and bearings (M) incorporate Variation but that Compass courses and bearings (C) involve Deviation in addition to Variation.

10 July 1975

1. 0600 depart Plymouth Breakwater Light. Wind N3 and visibility very good. Estimated speed of yacht 4 knots. Log 000.
   0730   Log 2.4   Plymouth Breakwater Light 033°M
                    Penlee Point Light 359°M
                    LHE Rame Head 303°M
   What is the 0730 fix?
2. 0730 a course of 285°C is set. Leeway 10°, and the boat's speed estimated at $4\frac{1}{2}$ knots.
   a.   What is the True course?
   b.   What is the 0800 EP?
3. 0800. In view of the forecast prospects of several hours of good weather with stable conditions the skipper decides to sail deeper into the bay. A course alteration of 316°C is made. Log reads 4.7. Leeway increased to 15° as the craft is now close-hauled. Estimated speed now 5 knots.
   What is the 0830 EP?
4. 0830   Log 7.1   RHE Rame Head 107°M
                    Beacon (50°20'.1N   04°13'.4W)   071°M
                    Beacon (50°21'.1N   04°16'.1W)   025°M
   a.   Plot the 0830 fix
   b.   'A good lookout is to be kept for them . . .' is a cautionary message printed on the chart. What does 'them' refer to?
   c.   A depth of 26 metres is recorded. What height of water is there above CD?
5. 0830 Engine switched on and course 011°C is steered. Estimated speed 5 knots.
   0850 Log 8.7. Skipper decides to anchor and do some fishing and he considers that a location between the 10m and 20m contour lines would be suitable. Yacht anchored in a position with the Beacon (50°21'.1N 04°16'.1W) bearing 055°M and the Tower at Portwrinkle bearing 325°M.
   a.   What is the True Course?
   b.   What is the position at the anchorage?
   c.   A depth (sounding) of 17 metres is recorded. How much water is there between CD and the bottom of the keel? (Don't forget that she draws 1.8 metres.)
6. 1040 Weigh anchor and set course 252°C. Log 8.7. The yacht is sailing on a broad reach with the wind still N but now dropped to force 2. Estimated speed 4 knots. Leeway nil.
   a.   What is the True Course?

Answers: Exercise 13

1. Since Looe HW time is only 5 minutes before the time in question, noon, then the Looe HW data will suffice.

Devonport HW time	1105 (G.M.T.)	Devonport HW height	4.3m
Looe difference	−0010	Looe difference	−0.2m
Looe HW time	1055 (G.M.T.)	Looe HW height	4.1m
	1155 (B.S.T.)	CD is	−0.3m
		Actual depth	3.8m

2.

Devonport HW time	2012 (G.M.T.)	Devonport LW time	1348 (G.M.T.)
Fowey difference	−0014	Fowey difference	−0009
Fowey HW time	1958 (G.M.T.)	Fowey LW time	1339 (G.M.T.)
	2058 (B.S.T.)		1439 (B.S.T.)
Devonport HW height	5.8	Devonport LW height	0.4
Fowey difference	−0.1	Fowey difference	−0.2
Fowey HW height	5.7m	Fowey LW height	0.2m
Fowey Range = 5.5m			

CD is given as 6.1m, so this subtracted from 8m gives the height above CD which we required: 1.9m. Now LW is 0.2m, so this taken away from 1.9m will leave us with the amount of the RANGE required. This is 1.7m.

	MHWS	MHWN	MLWN	MLWS
DEVONPORT	5.5	4.4	2.2	0.8
FOWEY differences	−0.1	−0.1	−0.2	−0.2
FOWEY heights	5.4	4.3	2.0	0.6

FOWEY MEAN RANGES   Mean Spring Range 4.8

Factor = $\dfrac{1.7}{5.5}$ = .31   Mean Neap Range 2.3

Entering Spring curve on graph, Factor .31 gives us −4 hours 17 minutes. 4 hours 17 minutes before 1958 G.M.T. is 1541 G.M.T. which is 1641 B.S.T.

Answers opposite

7. 1140 Portwrinkle Tower 052° LHE St George's Island 306°M Hill 154° (east of Looe) 351°M. Log 12.6. Leeway estimated at 10° and speed 4 knots. Wind NE 4.
   a. What is 1140 fix?
   b. What compass course would you steer in order to make good required track of 312°T (from 1140 fix to Looe Light) (Use ⬧ tidal streams?)
   c. What is the 1140 EP? (Use tidal streams between ⬧ and ⬧ .)
   b. What is the DR Pos. at 1140?

8. If the CD at Looe is −0.3m at the entrance, at what time during the afternoon could the craft be taken into Looe with a clearance at least 0.5 metres beneath her keel?
   What is the ETA (Estimated Time of Arrival) at Looe Light?

Answers: FINAL TEST PIECE

1. 033°M Variation 8°W   025°T
   359°M Variation 8°W   351°T
   303°M Variation 8°W   295°T
   0730 fix 50°17′.9N   04°11′W

2. a) 285°C Deviation 2°E 287°M Variation 8°W 279°T
   b) Leeway track 269°T (279° −10°). Take $2\frac{1}{4}$ miles (half an hour's run) along leeway track to get 0800 1st EP which is 50°17′.9N 04°14′.5W
   HW 10 July 1975 0631 G.M.T. (0731 B.S.T.) Springs.
   Work from ◇G◇
   0730 (at HW) 081° at 1.0 knots
   0830 (1 hour after HW) 111° at 0.8 knots
   0800 (midway between 0730 and 0830) 096° at 0.9 knots
   Stream 0730–0800 088° at 1.0 knots
   Use half an hour's drift of 088° at 1 knot (0.5 miles)
   0800 final EP 50°17′.9N   04°13′.8W

3. From the 0800 EP plot True course (316°C Deviation 1°W   315°M Variation 8°W   307°T).
   From the 0800 EP plot leeway track (292°T) and along it measure half an hour's run of vessel (2.5 miles) to get 0830 1st EP which is 50°18′.8N 04°17′.4W.
   0800 096° at 0.9 knots
   0830 111° at 0.8 knots
   Stream 0800-0830 103° at 0.9 knots
   Use half an hour's drift of 103° at 0.9 knots (0.5 miles)
   0830 final EP 50°18′.7N   04°16′.6W

4. a) 107°M Variation 8°W   099°T
   071°M Variation 8°W   063°T
   025°M Variation 8°W   017°T
   0830 fix 50° 19N   04°16′.9W
   b) Submarines
   c) Charted Depth is 23m so height above CD is 3m.

5. a) 011°C Deviation 3°W 008°M Variation 8°W 000°T
   b) 055°M Variation 8°W 047°T
   325°M Variation 8°W 317°T
   Anchorage position is 50°20′.6N 04°16′.9W
   c) Charted Depth 14.6m Sounding 17.0m
   Height above CD 2.4–1.8m draft leaves 0.6m.

6. a) 252°C Deviation 5°E   257°M   Variation 8°W   249°T
   1140 DR Pos. 50°19′.2N   04°22′.7W
   Since there is no leeway to bother about then only tidal streams are needed.
   Use mid way ◇F◇ and ◇G◇
   1040 (3 hours after HW) at ◇F◇ 136° at 0.4 knots
   1040 at ◇G◇ 235° at 0.3 knots
   1140 (4 hours after HW) at ◇F◇ 207° at 0.3 knots
   1140 at ◇G◇ 242° at 0.8 knots
   Stream 1040–1140 205° at 0.5 knots
   1140 EP 50°18′.7N   04°23′W

7. a. 1140 fix 50°18′.7N   04°23′W
    b) Plot required track, then the stream. It's about 3½ miles from 1140
        position to Looe Light so 1 hour's stream 1140–1240 will do.
        Use ⟨F⟩
        1140 (4 hours after HW) 207° at 0.3 knots
        1140–1240 stream 224° at 0.5 knots
        1240 (5 hours after HW) 241° at 0.6 knots
        Now you want the triangle of velocities. If you need reminding how to
        do this look at Fig. 10:5 on page 132. Counteract the stream first,
        then the leeway and then apply the Variation and Deviation for the
        course to steer to make good track 312°T. (This is 318°T + 10°
        leeway which is 328°T. Variation is 8°W and Deviation is 1°W. The
        compass course to steer is 337°C).
    c) Distance made good over the ground in 1 hour = 3.95 miles (use 4.0
        miles). Thus effective speed is about 4 knots. The exact distance
        from 1140 fix to Looe Light is 3.4 miles. 3.4 ÷ 4.0 = 0.85 hours
        (about 51 mins). ETA is 1140 + 51 minutes = 1231.
8. Draft 1.8m + clearance 0.5m + level below sea bed 0.3m = level
    required above CD (2.6m). From this take LW height of 0.5m and the
    level (height) needed above LW height is 2.1m. In other words we need
    2.1m of the total RANGE at Looe.

Devonport HW height	5.5	Devonport LW height	0.7
Looe difference	−0.1	Looe difference	−0.2
Looe HW height	5.4m	Looe LW height	0.5m

RANGE at Looe is 4.9m (5.4 − 0.5)

Devonport HW time	1850 G.M.T.
Looe difference	−0010
Looe HW time	1840 G.M.T. (1940 B.S.T.)
Devonport LW time	1235 G.M.T.
Looe difference	−0005
Looe LW time	1230 G.M.T. (1330 B.S.T.)

Looe Mean Spring range 4.8 (5.4 − 0.6)
Looe Mean Neap Range 2.2 (4.2 − 2.0)
– therefore we use Spring curve

$\dfrac{2.1}{4.9}$ = Factor .43

Entering graph at .43 we get −3 hours 50 minutes
1840 − 3 hours 50 minutes gives 1450 G.M.T. (1550 B.S.T.)

REFERENCES

The following works have been found helpful in the preparation of this book.

B. W. Lucke, *A Course On The Chart,* London, Pergamon Press, 1966.
A Seaman's Guide To Basic Chartwork, Bristol, ESL, 1970
Admiralty Tide Tables, Vol. 1, 1975. London, HMSO.
An Introduction To Coastal Navigation, Bristol, ESL, 1973.
Cruising Association Handbook, London, Cruising Association, 1971.
B. Anderson, *Navigation Exercises For Yachtsmen,* London, Stanford Maritime, 1974.
Reed's Nautical Almanac, 1975. London, Thomas Reed Publications Limited.
Symbols and Abbreviations 5011. London, HMSO.
A. C. Gardners, Teach Yourself Navigation, London, Hodder & Stoughton, 1970.
D. O. Harvey, *Yachting and Boating Book of Navigation,* London, Sphere, 1972.
Conrad Dixon, *Start to Navigate,* London, Adlard Coles Ltd, 1977.
J. Howard-Williams, *Practical Pilotage,* London, Adlard Coles Ltd, 1977.

INDEX